PRAYING
OF JESUS

PRAYING THE NAME
OF JESUS

[
the Ancient Wisdom
of the Jesus Prayer
]

Wilfrid Stinissen
Translated by Joseph B. Board, J.D., Ph.D.

Liguori

LIGUORI, MISSOURI

Published by Liguori Publications
Liguori, Missouri
http://www.liguori.org

Library of Congress Cataloging-in-Publication Data

Stinissen, Wilfrid 1927–.
  [Mitt namn är i dig. English]
  Praying the name of Jesus : the ancient wisdom of the Jesus prayer / Wilfrid Stinissen and a monk from the Eastern Church.
    p.   cm.
  Includes bibliographical references
  ISBN 0-7648-0496-0 (pbk.)
  1. Jesus Prayer. I. Moine de l'Eglise d'Orient, 1893–1980. On the invocation of the name of Jesus. II. Title.
BT590.J28S8513 1999
242'.7—dc21   99–33765

Printed in the United States of America
03 02 01 00 99 5 4 3 2 1
First Edition

Contents

Contents

PRAYING THE NAME
OF JESUS

PART I

On the Invocation
of the Name of Jesus

Foreword
to
Part I

The invocation of the Name of Jesus is a way of prayer perhaps more familiar to Christians of the East than of the West. In the Orthodox Church it is known under the name of the "Jesus Prayer" and it is widely practiced, not only in monasteries (e.g., on Mount Sinai and Mount Athos), but by lay people as well.[1] The invocation of the Holy Name, however, has also been used by many generations of Western Christians. It was propagated among them by saints like Bernard of Clairvaux (12th century) and Bernardino of Siena (14th century). This form of prayer has a universal appeal—to Orthodox and Romans, to Anglicans and Protestants, to all kinds of Christians of both Eastern and Western traditions. This is why its publication has been deemed in some manner appropriate by the Anglo-Orthodox Fellowship of St. Alban and St. Sergius.

This short work has a purely practical character. It has been written with the hope of giving a little help to Christians in the world—or even perhaps in the cloister—who desire to follow the "way of the Name." It is the outcome of twenty-five years of meditation and, so to speak, of inner experiment on the subject. Therefore it makes, we should not say difficult, but perhaps rather concentrated reading. We have tried always to remain as clear and simple as possible and to avoid theological technicalities. Yet the questions dealt with have a density of their own. However self-complacent this may sound, we ask those who will go over our pages not to hasten through them nor to read them all at once. The substance of the book would elude a hurried use of it—as sand runs between the fingers. This small treatise has been divided into chapters, and each chapter into numbered units. Every one of these distinct portions holds within its fixed limits a purpose and a meaning which should be gradually and fully taken in. We should be glad if our composition were read little by little, as a devotional booklet.

The English text owes much to the Rev. Frederick John Nash, and to Miss Helle Georgiadis and Miss Joan Ford, Secretaries of the Fellowship of St. Alban and St. Sergius. To them all we express our deep gratitude. The very fact that some Anglicans and Orthodox have been concerned with the author in bringing this work to its present state is a welcome sign of their common acknowledgment of the prayer described here as possessing a fundamental and universal Christian value.

We beg to be allowed to dedicate our little book both to the Fellowship of St. Alban and St. Sergius and to the Movement of Orthodox Youth of the Middle East.[2]

> O God, who didst appoint thine only be-
> gotten Son to be the Redeemer of mankind
> and didst command that his Name should
> be called Jesus: mercifully grant that we,
> who venerate his holy Name on earth, may
> likewise attain the fruition of beholding Him
> in heaven.[3]

> They that love thy Name shall be joyful in
> thee.[4]

London, St. Basil's House
February, 1949.

I

The Shape of the Invocation of the Name

And Jacob asked him and said:
"Tell me, I pray thee, thy name."
And he said: "Wherefore is it that thou
dost ask after my name?"
And he blessed him there.

Genesis 32:29

1 The invocation of the Name of Jesus can be put into many frames. It is for each person to find the form which is the most appropriate to his or her own prayer. But, whatever formula may be used, the heart and center of the invocation must be the Holy Name itself, the word *Jesus*. There resides the whole strength of the invocation.

2 The Name of Jesus may either be used alone or be inserted in a more or less developed phrase. In the East the commonest form is: "Lord Jesus Christ, Son of God, have mercy upon me, a sinner." One might simply say, "Jesus Christ" or "Lord Jesus." The invo-

cation may even be reduced to one single word, "Jesus."

3 This last form—the Name of Jesus only—is the most ancient mold of the invocation of the Name. It is the shortest, the simplest and, as we think, the easiest. Therefore, without deprecating the other formulas, we suggest that the word "Jesus" alone should be used.

4 Thus, when we speak of the invocation of the Name, we mean the devout and frequent repetition of the Name itself, of the word "Jesus" without additions. The Holy Name is the prayer.

5 The Name of Jesus may be either pronounced or silently thought. In both cases there is a real invocation of the Name, verbal in the first case, and purely mental in the second. This prayer affords an easy transition from verbal to mental prayer. Even the verbal repetition of the Name, if it is slow and thoughtful, makes us pass to mental prayer and disposes the soul to contemplation.

II

The Practice of the Invocation of the Name

And I will wait on thy name.
Psalm 52:9

6 The invocation of the Name may be practiced anywhere and at any time. We can pronounce the Name of Jesus in the streets, in the place of our work, in our room, in church, etc. We can repeat the Name while we walk. Besides that "free" use of the Name, not determined or limited by any rule, it is good to set apart certain times and certain places for a "regular" invocation of the Name. One who is advanced in that way of prayer may dispense with such arrangements. But they are an almost necessary condition for beginners.

7 If we daily assign a certain time to the invocation of the Name (besides the "free" invocation which should be as frequent as possible), the invocation ought to be practiced—circumstances allowing—in a lonely and quiet place: "Thou, when thou prayest, enter into thine inner chamber, and, when thou hast shut thy

door, pray to thy Father which is in secret."[1] The bodily posture does not matter much. One may walk, or sit down, or lie, or kneel. The best posture is the one which affords most physical quiet and inner concentration. One may be helped by a physical attitude expressing humbleness and worship.

8 Before beginning to pronounce the Name of Jesus, establish peace and recollection within yourself and ask for the inspiration and guidance of the Holy Ghost. "No man can say that Jesus is the Lord, but by the Holy Ghost."[2] The Name of Jesus cannot really enter a heart that is not being filled by the cleansing breath and the flame of the Spirit. The Spirit himself will breathe and light in us the Name of the Son.

9 Then simply begin. In order to walk one must take a first step; in order to swim one must throw oneself into the water. It is the same with the invocation of the Name. Begin to pronounce it with adoration and love. Cling to it. Repeat it. Do not think that you are invoking the Name; think only of Jesus himself. Say his Name slowly, softly, and quietly.

10 A common mistake of beginners is to wish to associate the invocation of the Holy Name with inner intensity or emotion. They try to say it with great force. But the Name of Jesus is not to be shouted, or fashioned with violence, even inwardly.

When Elijah was commanded to stand before the Lord, there was a great and strong wind, but the Lord was not in the wind; and after the wind an earthquake, but the Lord was not in the earthquake; and after the earthquake a fire, but the Lord was not in the fire. After the fire came a still small voice, "And it was so, when Elijah heard it, that he wrapped his face in his mantle, and went out, and stood...."[3] Strenuous exertion and the search for intensity will be of no avail. As you repeat the Holy Name, gather quietly, little by little, your thoughts and feelings and will around it; gather around it your whole being. Let the Name penetrate your soul as a drop of oil spreads out and impregnates a cloth. Let nothing of yourself escape. Surrender your whole self and enclose it within the Name.

11 Even in the act of invocation of the Name, its literal repetition ought not to be continuous. The Name pronounced may be extended and prolonged in seconds or minutes of silent rest and attention. The repetition of the Name may be likened to the beating of wings by which a bird rises into the air. It must never be labored and forced, or hurried, or in the nature of a flapping. It must be gentle, easy, and—let us give to this word its deepest meaning—graceful. When the bird has reached the desired height it glides in its flight, and only beats its wing from time to time in order to stay in the air. So the soul, having attained to the thought of Jesus and filled herself with

the memory of him, may discontinue the repetition of the Name and rest in Our Lord. The repetition will only be resumed when other thoughts threaten to crowd out the thought of Jesus. Then the invocation will start again in order to gain fresh impetus.

12 Continue this invocation for as long as you wish or as you can. The prayer is naturally interrupted by tiredness. Then do not insist. But resume it at any time and wherever you may be, when you feel again so inclined. In time you will find that the Name of Jesus will spontaneously come to your lips and almost continuously be present to your mind, though in a quiescent and latent manner. Even your sleep will be impregnated with the Name and memory of Jesus. "I sleep, but my heart waketh."[4]

13 When we are engaged in the invocation of the Name, it is natural that we should hope and endeavor to reach some "positive" or "tangible" result, i.e., to feel that we have established a real contact with the person of Our Lord: "If I may but touch his garment, I shall be whole."[5] This blissful experience is the desired climax of the invocation of the Name: "I will not let thee go, except thou bless me."[6] But we must avoid an overeager longing for such experiences: religious emotion may easily become a disguise for some dangerous kind of greed and sensuousness. Let us not think that, if we have spent a certain time

in the invocation of the Name without "feeling" anything, our time has been wasted and our effort unfruitful. On the contrary this apparently barren prayer may be more pleasing to God than our moments of rapture, because it is pure from any selfish quest for spiritual delight. It is the prayer of the plain and naked will. We should therefore persevere in assigning every day some regular and fixed time to the invocation of the Name, even if it seems to us that this prayer leaves us cold and dry; and such an earnest exertion of the will, such a sober "waiting" on the Name, cannot fail to bring us some blessing and strength.

14 Moreover, the invocation of the Name seldom leaves us in a state of dryness. Those who have some experience of it agree that it is very often accompanied by an inner feeling of joy, warmth, and light. One has an impression of moving and walking in the light. There is in this prayer no heaviness, no languishing, no struggling. "Thy name is as ointment poured forth....Draw me; we will run after thee."[7]

III

The Invocation of the Name as a Spiritual Way

I will strengthen them in the Lord, and
they shall walk up and down in his name.
Zechariah 10:12

15 The invocation of the Name of Jesus may be
simply an episode on our spiritual way (an
episode is, etymologically, something that happens "on
the way"). Or it may be for us *a* way, one spiritual
way among others. Or it may be *the* way, the spiritual
way which we definitely and predominantly (if not
exclusively) choose. In other terms the invocation of
the Name may be for us either a transitory act, a prayer
which we use for a time and leave it for others; or—
more than an act—a method which we continuously
use, but in addition to other forms and methods of
prayer; or the method around which we ultimately
build and organize our whole spiritual life. It all de-
pends on our personal call, circumstances, and possi-
bilities. Here we are only concerned with "beginners,"
with those who wish to acquire the first notions about
that prayer and a first contact with the Holy Name,

and also with those who, having had this first contact, wish to enter "the way of the Name." As to those who are already able to use the invocation of the Name as a method or as the only method, they do not need our advice.

16 We must not come to the invocation of the Name through some whim or arbitrary decision of our own. We must be called to it, led to it by God. If we try to use the invocation of the Name as our main spiritual method, this choice ought to be made out of obedience to a very special vocation. A spiritual practice and much more a spiritual system grounded on a mere caprice will miserably collapse. So we should be moved towards the Name of Jesus under the guidance of the Holy Spirit, then the invocation of the Name will be in us a fruit of the Spirit itself.

17 There is no infallible sign that we are called to the way of the Name. There may be, however, some indications of this call, which we ought to consider humbly and carefully. If we feel drawn towards the invocation of the Name, if this practice produces in us an increase of charity, purity, obedience, and peace, if the use of other prayers even is becoming somewhat difficult, we may, not unreasonably, assume that the way of the Name is open to us.

18 Anyone who feels the attraction of the way of the Name ought to be careful not to depreciate other forms of prayer. Let us not say: "The invocation of the Name is the best prayer." The best prayer is for everybody the prayer to which he or she is moved by the Holy Spirit, whatever prayer it may be. He who practices the invocation of the Name must also curb the temptation of an indiscreet and premature propaganda on behalf of this form of prayer. Let us not hasten to say to God: "I will declare thy name unto thy brethren,"[8] if he is not especially entrusting us with this mission. We should rather humbly keep the secrets of the Lord.

19 What we may say with soberness and truth is this. The invocation of the Name of Jesus simplifies and unifies our spiritual life. No prayer is simpler than this "one-word prayer" in which the Holy Name becomes the only focus of the whole life. Complicated methods often tire and dissipate thought. But the Name of Jesus easily gathers everything into itself. It has a power of unification and integration. The divided personality which could say: "My name is legion, for we are many"[9] will recover its wholeness in the sacred Name: "*Unite* my heart to fear thy name."[10]

20 The invocation of the Name of Jesus ought not to be understood as a "mystical way" which might spare us the ascetical purifications. There is no shortcut in spiritual life. The way of the Name implies a constant watch over our souls. Sin has to be avoided. There are only two possible attitudes in this respect. Some may guard their mind, memory, and will in order to say the Holy Name with greater recollection and love. Others will say the Holy Name in order to be more recollected and whole-hearted in their love. To our mind the latter is the better way. The Name itself is a means of purification and perfection, a touchstone, a filter through which our thoughts, words, and deeds have to pass to be freed from their impurities. None of them ought to be admitted by us until we pass them *through* the Name,—and the Name excludes all sinful elements. Only that will be received which is compatible with the Name of Jesus. We shall fill our hearts to the brim with the Name and thought of Jesus, holding it carefully, like a precious vessel, and defending it against all alien tampering and admixture. This is a severe asceticism. It requires a forgetfulness of self, a dying to self, as the Holy Name grows in our souls: "He must increase, but I must decrease."[11]

21 We have to consider the invocation of the Holy Name in relation to other forms of prayer. Of liturgical prayer and of the prayers fixed by some Community rule we shall say nothing, as we are only concerned here with individual and private prayer. We do not disparage or undervalue in the least

liturgical prayer and the prayers settled by obedience. Their corporate character and their very fixity render them extremely helpful. But it is for Churchmen and Community members to ascertain whether or how far the invocation of the Name of Jesus is compatible, in their own case, with the official formularies. Questions may be raised about some other forms of individual prayer. What about the "dialogue prayer," in which we listen and speak to God? What about the purely contemplative and wordless prayer, "prayer of quiet" and "prayer of union"? Must we leave these for the invocation of the Holy Name, or inversely? Or should we use both? The answer must be left for God to give in each individual case. In some rare cases the divine call to the invocation of the Name may be exclusive of all other forms of prayer. But we think that, generally speaking, the way of the Name is broad and free; it is, in most cases, perfectly compatible with moments of listening to the inner Word and answering it and with intervals of complete inner silence. Besides we must never forget that the best form of prayer which we can make at any given moment is that to which we are moved by the Holy Spirit.

22 The advice and discreet guidance of some spiritual "elder" who has a personal experience of the way of the Name may very often be found useful by the beginner. We personally would recommend resort to some such conductor. It is, however,

not indispensable. "When the Spirit of truth is come, he will guide you into all truth."[12]

IV

The Invocation of the Name as Worship

I will glorify thy name for evermore.
Psalm 86:12

23 We have considered until now the invocation of the Name of Jesus in a general manner. Now we must consider the diverse aspects of this invocation. The first aspect is adoration and worship.

24 Too often our prayers are limited to petition, intercession, and repentance. As we shall see the Name of Jesus can be used in all these ways. But the disinterested prayer, the praise given to God because of His own excellency, the regard directed towards Him with the utmost respect and affection, the exclamation of Thomas: "My Lord and my God!"— this ought to come first.

25 The invocation of the Name of Jesus must bring Jesus to our mind. The Name is the symbol and bearer of the Person of Christ. Otherwise the invocation of the Name would be mere verbal

idolatry. "The letter killeth, but the spirit giveth life."[13] The presence of Jesus is the real content and the substance of the Holy Name. The Name both signifies Jesus' presence and brings its reality.

26 This leads to pure adoration. As we pronounce the Name, we should respond to the presence of Our Lord. "They...fell down and worshiped him."[14] To pronounce thoughtfully the Name of Jesus is to know the allness of Our Lord and our own nothingness. In this knowledge we shall adore and worship. "God also hath highly exalted him and given him a name which is above every name: that at the name of Jesus every knee should bow."[15]

V

The Holy Name as a Mystery of Salvation

Save me, O God, by thy name.
Psalm 54:1

27 The Name of Jesus brings us more than his presence. Jesus is present in his Name as a Savior, for the word "Jesus" means just this: savior or salvation. "Neither is there salvation in any other; for there is no other name under heaven given among men, whereby we must be saved."[16] Jesus began his earthly mission by healing and forgiving, i.e., by saving men. In the same manner the very beginning of the way of the Name is the knowledge of Our Lord as our personal Savior. The invocation of the Name brings deliverance to us in all our necessities.

28 The Name of Jesus not only helps us to obtain the fulfillment of our needs ("Whatsoever ye shall ask the Father in my name, he will give it to you. Hitherto have ye asked nothing in my name: ask, and ye shall receive").[17] But the Name of Jesus already supplies our needs. When we require the suc-

cor of Our Lord we should pronounce his Name in
faith and hope, believing that we already receive in it
what we ask for. Jesus Himself is the supreme satisfaction of all men's needs. And He is that now, as we
pray. Let us not regard our prayer in relation to fulfillment in the future, but in relation to fulfillment *in
Jesus now*. He is more than the giver of what we and
others need. He is also the gift. He is both giver and
gift, containing in Himself all good things. If I hunger
he is my food. If I am cold he is my warmth. If I am ill
he is my health. If I am persecuted he is my deliverance. If I am impure he becomes my purity. He "is
made unto us...righteousness and sanctification and
redemption."[18] This is quite another thing than if he
had merely given them to us. Now we may find in his
Name all that he is. Therefore the Name of Jesus, in-
sofar as it links us with Jesus Himself, is already a
mystery of salvation.

29 The Name of Jesus brings victory and peace
when we are tempted. A heart already filled
with the Name and presence of Our Lord would not
let in any sinful image or thought. But we are weak,
and often our defenses break down, and then temptation rises within us like angry waters. In such case do
not consider the temptation, do not argue with your
own desire, do not think upon the storm, do not look
at yourself. Look at Our Lord, cling to Him, call upon
His Holy Name. When Peter, walking upon the waters

to come to Jesus, saw the tempest, "he was afraid"[19] and began to sink. If, instead of looking at the waves and listening to the wind, we single-heartedly walk upon the waters towards Jesus, He will stretch forth his hand and take hold of us. The Name may then be of great use, as it is a definite, concrete, and powerful shape able to resist the strong imagery of temptation. When tempted, call upon the Holy Name persistently, but quietly and gently. Do not shout it nor say it with anxiety or passion. Let it penetrate the soul little by little, till all thoughts and feelings come together and coalesce around it. Let it exercise its power of polarization. It is the Name of the Prince of Peace; it must be invoked in peace, and then it will bring us peace, or better still, it will (like Him whose symbol it is) be our peace.

30 The Name of Jesus brings forgiveness and reconciliation. When we have grievously sinned (and so much the more when we have sinned lightly), we can, within one second, cling to the Holy Name with repentance and charity and pronounce it with our whole heart, and the Name thus used (and through which we have reached the person of Christ) will already be a token of pardon. After sin let us not "hang about," delay, and linger. Let us not hesitate to take up again the invocation of the Name, in spite of our unworthiness. A new day is breaking and Jesus stands on the shore. "When Simon Peter heard that it was

the Lord he...cast himself into the sea."[20] Act like Simon. Say "Jesus," as though beginning life afresh. We sinners shall find our Lord anew at the invocation of His Name. He comes to us at that moment and as we are. He begins again where He has left us or, rather, where we have left Him. When He appeared to the disciples after the Resurrection, He came to them as they were—unhappy, and lost, and guilty—and without reproaching them with their past defection, He simply entered anew into their everyday life. "...He said unto them; 'Have ye here any meat?' And they gave him a piece of broiled fish and of an honeycomb."[21] In the same manner, when we say "Jesus" again, after an act of sin or a period of estrangement, He does not require from us long apologies for the past, but He wants us to mix, as before, His Person and His Name with the detail and routine of our life—with our broiled fish and our honeycomb—and to replunge them in the very middle of our existence.

31 Thus the Holy Name can bring about reconciliation after our actual sins. But it can give us a more general and fundamental experience of the divine forgiveness. We can pronounce the Name of Jesus and put into it the whole reality of the cross, the whole mystery of the atonement. If we link the Name with faith in Jesus as propitiation for the sins of all men, we find in the Holy Name the sign of the Redemption extended to all times and to the whole uni-

verse. Under this Name we find "the lamb slain from the foundation of the world,"[22] "the lamb of God which taketh away the sin of the world."[23]

32 All this does not gainsay or tend to lessen the objective means of penitence and remission of sins offered to us by the Church. We are here only concerned with the hidden life of the soul. What we have in view is the inner absolution which repentance produced by charity already obtains—the absolution which the publican received after his prayer in the temple and of which the Gospel says: "This man went down to his house justified."[24]

$$\overline{\text{VI}}$$

The Name of Jesus
and the Incarnation

And the Word became flesh.
John 1:14

33 We have considered the "saving" power of the Holy Name; we must now go further. In proportion as the Name of Jesus grows within us, we grow in the knowledge of the divine mysteries. The Holy Name is not only a mystery of salvation, the fulfillment of our needs, the abatement of our temptations, the forgiveness of our sins. The invocation of the Name is also a means of applying to ourselves the mystery of the Incarnation. It is a powerful means of union with Our Lord. To be united to Christ is even more blessed than to stand before Him or to be saved through Him. Union is greater than presence and meditation.

34 You may pronounce the Name of Jesus in order "that Christ may dwell in your hearts."[25] You may, when this Name is formed on your lips, experience the reality of His coming in the soul:

"I stand at the door and knock; if any man hear my voice, and open the door, I will come in to him, and will sup with him, and he with me."[26] You may enthrone His Person and His Name, as signifying the Person, within yourselves: "They have built Thee a sanctuary therein for Thy name."[27] It is the "I in them" of Our Lord's priestly prayer.[28] Or we may throw ourselves into the Name and feel that we are the members of the Body of Christ and the branches of the true vine. "Abide in me."[29] Of course, nothing can abolish the difference between the Creator and the creature. But there is, made possible by the Incarnation, a real union of mankind and of our own persons with Our Lord,—a union which the use of the Name of Jesus may express and strengthen.

35 Some analogy exists between the Incarnation of the Word and the indwelling of the Holy Name within us. The Word was made flesh. Jesus became man. The inner reality of the Name of Jesus, having passed into our souls, overflows into our bodies. "Put ye on the Lord Jesus Christ."[30] The living content of the Name enters physically into ourselves. "Thy Name is as ointment poured forth."[31] The Name, if I repeat it with faith and love, becomes a strength able to paralyze and overcome "the law of sin which is in my members."[32] We can also put on ourselves the Name of Jesus as a kind of physical seal keeping our hearts and bodies pure and consecrated. "Set me as a

seal upon thine heart, as a seal upon thine arm."[33] But this physical seal is not a piece of wax or lead. It is the outward sign and the Name of the living Word.

VII

The Name of Jesus
and Transfiguration

**...The fullness of Him that filleth
all in all.**
Ephesians 1:23

36 The use of the Holy Name not only brings
anew the knowledge of our own union with
Jesus in His Incarnation. The Name is also an instrument by which we may obtain a wider view of Our
Lord's relation to all that God has made. The Name
of Jesus helps us to transfigure the world into Christ
(without any pantheistic confusion). Here is another
aspect of the invocation of the Name: it is a method
of transfiguration.

37 It is so in regard to nature. The natural universe may be considered as the handiwork
of the Creator: "...the Lord that made heaven and
earth."[34] It can be considered as the visible symbol of
the invisible divine beauty: "The heavens declare the
glory of God."[35] "Consider the lilies of the field...."[36]
And yet all this is insufficient. Creation is not static. It

moves, striving and groaning, towards Christ as its fulfillment and end. "The whole creation groaneth and travaileth in pain"[37] till it be "delivered from the bondage of corruption into the glorious liberty of the children of God."[38] What we call the inanimate world is carried along by a Christward movement. All things were converging towards the Incarnation. The natural elements and the products of the earth, rock and wood, water and oil, corn and wine, were to acquire a new meaning and to become signs and means of grace. All creation mysteriously utters the Name of Jesus: "I tell you that, if these should hold their peace, the stones would immediately cry out."[39] It is the utterance of this Name that Christians should hear in nature. By pronouncing the Name of Jesus upon the natural things, upon a stone or a tree, a fruit or a flower, the sea or a landscape, or whatever it is, the believer speaks aloud the secret of these things, he brings them to their fulfillment, he gives an answer to their long and apparently dumb awaiting. "For the earnest expectation of the creature waiteth for the manifestation of the sons of God."[40] We shall say the Name of Jesus in union with all creation: "...at the name of Jesus every knee should bow, of things in heaven and things in earth and things under the earth...."[41]

38 The animal world may also be transfigured by us. When Jesus remained forty days in the wilderness, he "was with the wild beasts."[42] We do not know what happened then, but we may be assured that no living creature is left untouched by Jesus' influence. Jesus himself said of the sparrows that "not one of them is forgotten before God."[43] We are like Adam when he had to give a name to all the animals. "Out of the ground the Lord God formed every beast of the field, and every fowl of the air, and brought them unto Adam to see what he would call them."[44] Scientists call them as they think fit. As to us, if we invoke the Name of Jesus upon the animals, we give them back their primitive dignity which we so easily forget—the dignity of living beings being created and cared for by God in Jesus and for Jesus, "That was the name thereof."[45]

39 It is mainly in relation to men that we can exercise a ministry of transfiguration. The risen Christ appeared several times under an aspect which was no longer the one his disciples knew. "He appeared in another form…";[46] the form of a traveler on the road to Emmaus, or of a gardener near the tomb, or of a stranger standing on the shore of the lake. It was each time in the form of an ordinary man such as we may meet in our everyday life. Jesus thus illustrated an important aspect of his presence among us—his presence in man. He was thus completing what he had taught: "I was an hungred and ye gave me meat. I was thirsty and ye gave me drink…naked and

ye clothed me. I was sick, and ye visited me. I was in prison, and ye came unto me....Inasmuch as ye have done it unto one of the least of these my brethren, ye have done it unto me."[47] Jesus appears now to us under the features of men and women. Indeed this human form is now the only one under which everybody can, at will, at any time and in any place, see the Face of Our Lord. Men of today are realistically minded; they do not live on abstractions and phantoms; and, when the saints and the mystics come and tell them: "We have seen the Lord," they answer with Thomas: "Except I shall...put my finger into the print of the nails and thrust my hand into his side, I will not believe."[48] Jesus accepts this challenge. He allows Himself to be seen, and touched, and spoken to in the person of all his human brethren and sisters. To us as to Thomas He says: "Reach hither thy hand and thrust it into my side, and be not faithless, but believing."[49] Jesus shows us the poor, and the sick, and the sinners, and generally all men, and tells us: "Behold my hands and my feet....Handle me and see; for a spirit hath not flesh and bones, as ye see me have."[50] Men and women are the flesh and bones, the hands and feet, the pierced side of Christ—His mystical Body. In them we can experience the reality of the Resurrection and the real presence (though without confusion of essence) of the Lord Jesus. If we do not see Him, it is because of our hard-heartedness: "Their eyes were holden that they should not know Him."[51] Now the Name of Jesus is a

concrete and powerful means of transfiguring men into
their hidden, innermost, utmost reality. We should approach all men and women—in the street, the shop,
the office, the factory, the 'bus, the queue, and especially those who seem irritating and antipathetic—with
the Name of Jesus in our heart and on our lips. We
should pronounce His Name over them all, for their
real name is the Name of Jesus. Name them with his
Name, within His Name, in a spirit of adoration, dedi-
cation, and service. Adore Christ in them, serve Christ
in them. In many of these men and women—in the
malicious, in the criminal—Jesus is imprisoned. Deliver Him by silently recognizing and worshiping Him
in them. If we go through the world with this new
vision, saying "Jesus" over every man, seeing Jesus in
every man, everybody will be transformed and transfigured before our eyes. The more we are ready to
give of ourselves to men, the more will the new vision
be clear and vivid. The vision cannot be severed from
the gift. Rightly did Jacob say to Esau, when they were
reconciled: "I pray thee, if now I have found grace in
thy sight, then receive my present at my hand, for therefore have seen thy face as though I had seen the face
of God."[52]

VIII

The Name of Jesus and the Church

...to gather together in one all things in Christ, both which are in heaven and which are in earth....

Ephesians 1:10

40 In pronouncing the Name of Jesus we inwardly meet all them that are united with Our Lord, all them of whom He said: "Where two or three are gathered together in my name, there am I in the midst of them."[53]

41 We should find all men in the heart of Jesus and in His love. We should throw all men into His Name and enclose them therein. Long lists of intercessions are not necessary. We may *apply* the Name of Jesus to the name of such or such person who is in particular need. But all men and all just causes are already gathered together within the Name of Our Lord. Adhering to Jesus is to become one with Him in His solicitude and loving kindness for them. Adhering to Our Lord's own intercession for them is better than to plead with Him on their behalf.

42 Where Jesus is, there is the Church. Whoever is in Jesus is in the Church. If the invocation of the Holy Name is a means of union with Our Lord, it is also a means of union with that Church which is in Him and which no human sin can touch. This does not mean that we are closing our eyes to the problems of the Church on earth, to the imperfections and disunity of Christians. But we only deal here with this eternal, and spiritual, and "unspotted" side of the Church which is implied in the Name of Jesus. The Church thus considered transcends all earthly reality. No schism can rend her. Jesus said to the Samaritan woman: "Believe me, the hour cometh, when ye shall neither in this mountain, nor yet at Jerusalem, worship the Father....The hour cometh, and now is, when the true worshipers shall worship the Father in spirit and in truth."[54] There is an apparent contradiction in the words of Our Lord: how could the hour be still coming and yet already be? This paradox finds its explanation in the fact that the Samaritan woman was then standing before Christ. On the one hand the historical opposition between Jerusalem and Garizim still existed, and Jesus, far from treating it as a trifling circumstance, emphasized the higher claims of Jerusalem: "Ye worship ye know not what. We know what we worship: for salvation is of the Jews."[55] In that

sense the hour was not yet, but was still coming. On the other hand the hour already was, because the woman had before her Him who is greater than Jerusalem or Garizim, Him who "will tell us all things"[56] and in Whom alone we can fully "worship in spirit and in truth."[57] The same situation arises when, invoking the Name of Jesus, we cling to His Person. Assuredly we do not believe that all the conflicting interpretations of the Gospel which we hear on earth are equally true nor that the divided Christian groups have the same measure of light. But, fully pronouncing the Name of Jesus, entirely surrendered to His Person and His claims, we implicitly share in the wholeness of the Church, and so we experience her essential unity, deeper than all our human separations.

43 The invocation of the Name of Jesus helps us to meet again, in Him, all our departed. Martha was wrong when, speaking of Lazarus, she said to Our Lord: "I know that he shall rise again in the resurrection at the last day."[58] Overlooking the present she was projecting all her faith into the future. Jesus corrected her mistake: "I *am* the resurrection and the life."[59] The life and the resurrection of the departed is not merely a future event (although the resurrection of the individual bodies is such). The Person of the risen Christ already is the resurrection and the life of all men. Instead of trying to establish—in our prayer, or in our memory, or in our imagina-

tion—a direct spiritual contact with our departed, we should try to reach them within Christ, where their true life now is. One can, therefore, say that the invocation of the Name of Jesus is the best prayer for the departed. The invocation of the Name, giving us the presence of Our Lord, makes them also present to us. And our linking of the Holy Name with their own names is our work of love on their behalf.

44 These departed, whose life is now hidden with Christ, form the heavenly Church. They belong to the total and eternal Church, of which the Church now militant on earth is but a very small part. We meet in the Name of Jesus the whole company of the saints: "His Name shall be in their foreheads."[60] In it we meet the angels; it is Gabriel who, first on earth, announced the Holy Name, saying to Mary: "Thou shalt call his name Jesus."[61] In it we meet the woman "blessed among women" to whom Gabriel spoke these words and who so often called her son by His Name. May the Holy Spirit make us desire to hear the Name of Jesus as the Virgin Mary first heard it and to repeat that Name as Mary and Gabriel uttered it! May our own invocation of the Name enter this abyss of adoration, obedience, and tenderness!

IX

The Name of Jesus
as Eucharist

This do in remembrance of me.
Luke 22:19

45 The mystery of the Upper Room was a summing-up of the whole life and mission of Our Lord. The sacramental Eucharist lies outside the scope of the present considerations. But there is a "eucharistic" use of the Name of Jesus in which all the aspects which we have seen till now are gathered and unified.

46 Our soul also is an Upper Room where an invisible Lord's Supper may be celebrated at any time. Our Lord secretly tells us, as of old: "With desire I have desired to eat this passover with you[62]...Where is the guest-chamber where I shall eat the passover with my disciples?[63]...There make ready."[64] These words do not solely apply to the visible Lord's Supper. They also apply to his interior Eucharist, which, though only spiritual is very real. In the visible Eucharist, Jesus is offered under the signs of bread and wine. In the Eucharist within us He can be signified and designated by His Name alone. Therefore the invocation of the Holy Name may be made by us a Eucharist.

47 The original meaning of "eucharist" is: thanksgiving. Our inner Lord's Supper will first be a thanksgiving over the great gift—the gift made to us by the Father in the Person of His Son. "By Him…let us offer the sacrifice of praise to God continually…."[65] The Scripture immediately explains the nature of this sacrifice of praise: "…that is, the fruit of our lips giving thanks to His name." So the idea of the Name is linked with that of thanksgiving. Not only may we, while pronouncing Jesus' Name, thank the Father for having given us His Son or direct our praise towards the Name of the Son Himself, but we may make of the Name of the Son the substance and support of the sacrifice of praise rendered to the Father, the expression of our gratitude and our offering of thanks.

48 Every Eucharist is an offering. "That they may offer unto the Lord an offering in righteousness."[66] We cannot offer to the Father a better offering than the person of His Son Jesus. This offering alone is worthy of the Father. Our offering of Jesus to His Father is one with the offering which Jesus is eternally making of Himself, for how could we, alone,

offer Christ? In order to give a concrete shape to our offering we shall probably find it helpful to pronounce the Name of Jesus. We shall present the Holy Name to God as though it were bread and wine.

49 The Lord, in His Supper, offered to His disciples bread which was broken and wine which was shed. He offered a life which was given, His body and blood ready for the immolation. When we inwardly offer Jesus to His Father, we shall always offer Him as a victim—both slain and triumphant: "Worthy is the Lamb that was slain to receive… honour, and glory, and blessing."[67] Let us pronounce the Name of Jesus with the awareness that we are washed and made "white in the blood of the Lamb."[68] This is the sacrificial use of the Holy Name. This does not mean that we think of a new sacrifice of the cross. The Holy Name, sacrificially used, is but a means to apply to us, here and now, the fruits of the oblation once for all made and perfect. It helps us, in the exercise of the universal priesthood, to make spiritually actual and present the eternal sacrifice of Christ. The sacrificial use of the Name of Jesus will also remind us that we cannot be one with Jesus, priest and victim, if we do not offer within Him, within His Name, our own soul and body: "In burnt offerings and sacrifices for sin thou hast had no pleasure: Then said I, Lo, I come."[69]

50 There is no Lord's Supper without a communion. Our inner Eucharist also is what tradition has called "spiritual communion," that is, a feeding by faith on the Body and Blood of Christ without using the visible elements of bread and wine. "The bread of God is he which cometh down from heaven, and giveth life unto the world...I am that bread of life."[70] Jesus always remains the bread of life which we can receive as a food, even when we do not partake of any sacramental elements: "It is the spirit that quickeneth; the flesh profiteth nothing."[71] We can have a purely spiritual and invisible access to the Body and Blood of Christ. This inner, but very real, mode of approach to Our Lord is something distinct from any other approach to His Person, for here is a special gift and benefit, a special grace, a special relationship between Our Lord, as both feeder and food, and ourselves partaking (though invisibly) of that food. Now this spiritual communion of the divine Bread of life, of the Body and Blood of the Savior, becomes easier when it is given expression in the Holy Name, receiving from the Name of Jesus its shape, its frame and support. We can pronounce the Name of Our Lord with the special intention of feeding our soul on it, or rather on the sacred Body and precious Blood which we try to approach through it. Such a communion may be renewed as often as we desire. Far from us the error of treating lightly or lowering in esteem the Lord's Supper as practiced in the Church. But it is to be hoped

that everybody who follows the way of the Name may experience that the Name of Jesus is a spiritual food and communicates to hungry souls the Bread of life. "Lord, evermore give us this bread."[72] In this bread, in this Name, we find ourselves united with all them that share in the same Messianic meal: "We being many are one bread and one body: for we are all partakers of that one bread."[73]

51 Through the Eucharist we "do shew the Lord's death till he come."[74] The Eucharist is an anticipation of the eternal kingdom. The "eucharistic" use of the name of Jesus leads us to its "eschatological" use, that is, to the invocation of the Name in connection with the "end" and with the Coming of Our Lord. Each invocation of the Holy Name should be an ardent aspiration to our final reunion with Jesus in the heavenly kingdom. Such an aspiration is related to the end of the world and the triumphal Coming of Christ, but it has a nearer relation to the occasional (and, as we should ask, more and more frequent) breakings in of Christ into our earthly existence, His wonderful forcible entrances into our everyday life, and still more to the Coming of Christ to us at the time of our death. There is a way of saying "Jesus" which is a preparation for death, an aspiration towards death conceived as the long-expected appearing of the Friend "whom having not seen, ye love,"[75] a call for this supreme meeting and here and now a throwing of

our heart beyond the barrier. In that way of saying "Jesus," the longing utterance of Paul, "When Christ, who is our life, shall appear…"[76] and the cry of John, "Come, Lord Jesus,"[77] are already implied.

The Name of Jesus and the Holy Spirit

I saw the Spirit descending from heaven like a dove, and it abode upon him.
John 1:32

52 The Name of Jesus occupied a pre-eminent place in the message and action of the Apostles. They were preaching in the Name of Jesus, healing the sick in His Name; they were saying to God: "Grant unto thy servants...that signs and wonders may be done by the name of thy holy child Jesus."[78] Through them "the name of the Lord Jesus was magnified."[79] It is only after Pentecost that the Apostles announced the Name "with power." Jesus had told them: "Ye shall receive power, after that the Holy Ghost is come upon you."[80] In this "Pentecostal" use of the Name of Jesus we find clear evidence of the link between the Spirit and the Name. Such a Pentecostal use of the Name is not restricted to the Apostles. It is not only of the Apostles, but of all "them that believe," that Jesus said: "In my name they shall cast out devils; they shall speak with new tongues...they

shall lay hands on the sick, and they shall recover."[81] Only our lack of bold faith and charity prevents us from calling upon the Name in the power of the Spirit. If we really follow the way of the Name, a time must come when we become able (without pride, without looking at ourselves) to manifest the glory of Our Lord and to help other men through "signs." He whose heart is become a vessel of the Holy Name should not hesitate to go about and repeat to those who need spiritual or bodily relief the words of Peter: "Silver and gold have I none; but such as I have give I thee: in the name of Jesus Christ of Nazareth rise up and walk."[82] O that the Spirit of Pentecost may come and write within us the Name of Jesus in flame!

53 The Pentecostal use of the Name is but one aspect of our approach to the Holy Ghost through the Name of Jesus. The Name will lead us to some other and more inward experiences of the Spirit. While pronouncing the Name we may obtain a glimpse of the relationship between the Spirit and Jesus. There is a certain attitude of the Spirit towards Jesus and a certain attitude of Jesus towards the Spirit. In repeating the Name of Jesus we find ourselves at the crossroads, so to speak, where these two "movements" meet.

54 When Jesus was baptized "the Holy Ghost descended in bodily shape like a dove upon

Him."[83] The descent of the dove is the best expression of the attitude of the Spirit towards Our Lord. Now let us, while saying the Name of Jesus, try to coincide, if we may say so, with the Jesus-ward movement of the Spirit, with the Spirit directed by the Father towards Jesus, looking to Jesus, coming to Jesus. Let us try to unite ourselves—as much as a creature can unite itself to a divine action—to this flight of the dove ("Oh that I had wings like a dove..."[84]) and to the tender feelings expressed by her voice: "The voice of the turtle is heard in our land."[85] Before making "intercession for us with groanings which cannot be uttered,"[86] the Spirit was and eternally remains sighing after Jesus. The Book of Revelation shows us the Spirit, together with the Bride (that is, the Church), crying to Our Lord. When we utter the Name of Jesus, we can conceive it as the sigh and aspiration of the Holy Ghost, as the expression of the Spirit's desire and yearning. We shall thus be admitted (according to our feeble human capacity) into the mystery of the loving relationship between the Holy Ghost and the Son.

55 Conversely, the Name of Jesus may also help us to coincide with the attitude of Our Lord towards the Spirit. Jesus was conceived in Mary "of the Holy Ghost."[87] He remained during His whole earthly life (and still remains) the perfect receiver of the Gift, He let the Spirit take complete possession of Him, being "led up of the Spirit"[88] or driven by it. He

cast out devils "by the Spirit of God."[89] He returned from the desert "in the power of the Spirit."[90] He declared: "The Spirit of the Lord is upon me."[91] In all this Jesus shows a humble docility towards the Holy Ghost. In pronouncing the Name of Jesus we can (as far as is given to man) make ourselves one with Him in this surrender to the Spirit. But we can also make ourselves one with Him as with the starting point from which the Spirit is sent to men: "He shall take of mine, and shall shew it unto you[92]...I will send him unto you."[93] We can see the Name of Jesus as the focus from which the Spirit radiates towards mankind; we can see Jesus as the mouth from which the Spirit is breathed. Thus, in the utterance of the Name of Jesus, we can associate ourselves with these two moments: the filling of Jesus with the Spirit, the sending of the Spirit by Jesus. To grow in the invocation of the Holy Name is to grow in the knowledge of the "Spirit of his Son."[94]

XI

The Name of Jesus
and the Father

**He that hath seen me hath
seen the Father.**
John 14:9

56 Our reading of the Gospel will remain superficial as long as we only see in it a message directed to men or a life turned towards men. The very heart of the Gospel is the hidden relationship of Jesus with the Father. The secret of the Gospel is Jesus turned towards Him. This is the fundamental mystery of the life of Our Lord. The invocation of the Name of Jesus may afford us some real, though faint and transient, partaking in that mystery.

57 "In the beginning was the Word."[95] The Person of Jesus is the living Word spoken eternally by the Father. As the Name of Jesus, by a special divine dispensation, has been chosen to mean the living Word uttered by the Father, we may say that this Name partakes to some extent in this eternal utterance. In a somewhat anthropomorphic manner (easy to correct), we might say that the Name of Jesus is the only human word which the Father eternally pronounces. The Father eternally begets His Word. He gives Himself eternally in the begetting of the Word. If we endeavor to approach the Father through the invocation of the Name of Jesus, we have first, while pronouncing the Name, to contemplate Jesus as the object of the Father's love and self-giving. We have to feel (in our little way) the outpouring of this love and this gift on the Son. We have already seen the dove descending upon Him. It remains to hear the Father's voice saying: "Thou art my beloved son; in thee I am well pleased."[96]

58 And now we must humbly enter into the filial consciousness of Jesus. After having in the word "Jesus" the Father's utterance: "My son!", we ought to find in it the Son's utterance: "My Father!" Jesus has no other aim than to declare the Father and be His Word. Not only have all Jesus' actions, during His earthly life, been acts of perfect obedience to the Father ("My meat is to do the will of him that sent me"[97]); not only has the sacrificial death of Jesus fulfilled the supreme requirement of the divine love (of which the Father is the source): "Greater love hath no man than this, that a man lay down his life..."[98]— not only the deeds of Jesus, but His whole being were the perfect expression of the Father. Jesus is "the brightness of his glory, and image of his person."[99] The Word was "towards God"[100]—the translation

"with God" is inaccurate. It is this eternal orientation of the Son towards the Father, his eternal turning to Him, which we should experience within the Name of Jesus. There is more in the Holy Name than the "turning to" the Father. In saying "Jesus" we can in some measure join together the Father and the Son, we can realize and appropriate their oneness. At the very moment when we utter the Holy Name, Jesus Himself says to us as He said to Philip: "Believest thou not that I am in the Father and the Father in me?...Believe me that I am in the Father, and the Father in me."[101]

XII

The Name and
the Total Presence

**...that ye may be filled
unto all the fullness....**
Ephesians 3:19

59 We have considered the main aspects of the invocation of the Name of Jesus. We have disposed them according to a kind of ascending scale, and we think that this scale corresponds to the normal progress of the life of the soul. Nevertheless, God, who "giveth not the Spirit by measure,"[102] overpasses all our limits. These aspects of the Name intermingle; a beginner may straightway be raised to the highest perception of the content of the Name, while somebody who has been waiting on the Name for years may not go beyond the elementary stages (it is not this that matters, the only thing that matters is to do what Our Lord wants us to do). So the pattern which we have followed is, to a large extent, artificial and has but a relative value.

60 This becomes quite evident to anybody who has had some experience of all the aspects of the Name which have been described here. At that stage—the reaching of which does not necessarily imply a greater perfection, but often some intellectual and spiritual acumen, some quickness of perception and discrimination concerning the things of God—it becomes difficult, even wearisome and tedious, and sometimes even impossible, to concentrate on this or that particular aspect of the Name of Jesus, however lofty it may be. Our invocation and consideration of the Holy Name then becomes global. We become simultaneously aware of all the implications of the Name. We say "Jesus," and we are resting in the fullness and totality of the Name of Our Lord; we are unable to disjoin and isolate its diverse aspects, and yet we feel that all of them are there, as a united whole. The Holy Name is then bearing the whole Christ and introduces us to His total Presence.

61 This total Presence is more than the Presence of proximity and the Presence of indwelling of which we have already spoken. It is the actual "givenness" of all the realities to which the Name may have been for us an approach: Salvation, Incarnation, Transfiguration, Church, Eucharist, Spirit, and Father. It is then that we apprehend "what is the breadth and length and depth and height..."[103] and that we per-

ceive what to "gather together in one all things in Christ"[104] means.

62 This total Presence is all. The Name is nothing without the Presence. He who is able constantly to live in the total Presence of Our Lord does not need the Name. The Name is only an incentive and a support to the Presence. A time may come, even here on earth, when we have to discard the Name itself and to become free from everything but the nameless and unutterable living contact with the Person of Jesus.

63 When we separately consider the aspects or implications of the Name of Jesus, our invocation of the Name is like a prism which splits up a beam of white light into the several colors of the spectrum. When we call on the "total Name" (and the total Presence) we are using the Name as a lens which receives and concentrates the white light. Through the means of a lens a ray of the sun can ignite some combustible substance. The Holy Name is this lens. Jesus is the burning Light which the Name, acting as a lens, can gather and direct till a fire is kindled within us. "I am come to send fire on the earth...."[105]

64 The Scripture often promises a special blessing to them that call on the Name of the Lord. We may apply to the Name of Jesus what is said of

the Name of God. We shall therefore repeat: "Look thou upon me, and be merciful unto me, as thou usest to do unto those that love thy name."[106] And of every one of us may the Lord say what he said of Saul: "He is a chosen vessel unto me, to bear my name...."[107]

AMEN.

Notes from the Foreword

1. In a previous work entitled *Orthodox Spirituality, An Outline of the Orthodox ascetical and mystical Tradition* (S.P.C.K. London), we have pointed out (pp. 20–21) the importance of this form of prayer within the frame of Orthodox piety. We have since given a history and a bibliography of the subject in two articles, La *Priere de Jésus, Sa gènese et son développement dans la tradition spirituelle byzantino-slave,* published in the periodical *Irénikon* (Benedictine Priory of Amay, Chevetogne, Belgium), V. XX, 1947, pp. 249–273 and 381–421 [now available in an English translation: *The Prayer of Jesus,* by a Monk of the Eastern Church (Desclee Company, 1967)] See also N. Gorodetzky, *The Prayer of Jesus,* in *Blackfriars,* February, 1942, pp. 74–78, and *The Way of a Pilgrim,* anonymous, translated from the Russian by R. M. French (London, 1943). It must be made quite clear that the present considerations are dealing with the invocation of the Name of Jesus in a general way and not with the special formulas and methods of the Byzantine Jesus Prayer.
2. The headquarters of which are in Beirut (Lebanon).
3. Roman Missal, collect for the feast of the Holy Name of Jesus.
4. Psalm 5:12.

Biblical References

<table>
<tr><td>1. Matthew 6:6</td><td>18. 1 Corinthians 1:30</td></tr>
<tr><td>2. 1 Corinthians 12:3</td><td>19. Matthew 14:30</td></tr>
<tr><td>3. 1 Kings 19:13</td><td>20. John 21:7</td></tr>
<tr><td>4. Song of Songs 5:2</td><td>21. Luke 24:41–42</td></tr>
<tr><td>5. Matthew 9:21</td><td>22. Revelation 13:8</td></tr>
<tr><td>6. Genesis 32:26</td><td>23. John 1:29</td></tr>
<tr><td>7. Song of Songs 1:3–4</td><td>24. Luke 18:24</td></tr>
<tr><td>8. Psalm 22:22</td><td>25. Ephesians 3:17</td></tr>
<tr><td>9. Mark 5:9</td><td>26. Revelation 3:20</td></tr>
<tr><td>10. Psalm 86:11</td><td>27. 2 Chronicles 20:8</td></tr>
<tr><td>11. John 3:30</td><td>28. John 17:26</td></tr>
<tr><td>12. John 16:13</td><td>29. John 15:4</td></tr>
<tr><td>13. 2 Corinthians 3:6</td><td>30. Romans 13:14</td></tr>
<tr><td>14. Matthew 2:11</td><td>31. Song of Songs 1:3</td></tr>
<tr><td>15. Philippians 2:9–10</td><td>32. Romans 7:23</td></tr>
<tr><td>16. Acts 4:12</td><td>33. Song of Songs 8:6</td></tr>
<tr><td>17. John 16:23–24</td><td>34. Psalm 134:3</td></tr>
</table>

35. Psalm 19:1	57. John 4:24
36. Matthew 6:28	58. John 11:24
37. Romans 8:22	59. John 11:25
38. Romans 8:21	60. Revelation 22:4
39. Luke 19:40	61. Luke 1:31
40. Romans 8:19	62. Luke 22:15
41. Philippians 2:10	63. Luke 22:11
42. Mark 1:13	64. Luke 22:12
43. Luke 12:6	65. Hebrews 13:15
44. Genesis 2:19	66. Malachi 3:3
45. Genesis 2:19	67. Revelation 5:12
46. Mark 16:12	68. Revelation 7:14
47. Matthew 25:35–36, 40	69. Hebrews 10:6–7
48. John 20:25	70. John 6:33, 48
49. John 20:27	71. John 6:63
50. Luke 24:39	72. John 6:34
51. Luke 24:16	73. 1 Corinthians 10:17
52. Genesis 33:10	74. 1 Corinthians 11:26
53. Matthew 18:20	75. 1 Peter 1:8
54. John 4:21, 23	76. Colossians 3:4
55. John 4:22	77. Revelation 22:20
56. John 4:25	78. Acts 4:29, 30

79. Acts 19:17	94. Galatians 4:6
80. Acts 1:8	95. John 1:1
81. Mark 16:17–18	96. Luke 3:22
82. Acts 3:6	97. John 4:34
83. Luke 3:22	98. John 15:13
84. Psalm 55:6	99. Hebrews 1:3
85. Song of Songs 2:12	100. John 1:1
86. Romans 8:26	101. John 14:10, 11
87. Matthew 1:20	102. John 3:34
88. Matthew 4:1	103. Ephesians 3:18
89. Matthew 12:28	104. Ephesians 1:10
90. Luke 4:14	105. Luke 12:49
91. Luke 4:18	106. Psalm 119:132
92. John 16:15	107. Acts 9:15
93. John 16:7	

On Praying
the Name of Jesus

Foreword
to
Part II

For me, personally, the Jesus Prayer has received a greater place now than it had when this writing was first published almost twenty years ago. The simple repetition of the holy name, gladly in harmony with the body, seems to me more and more to be the fundamental point of departure for Christian inner prayer, the point to which the prayer constantly returns and where it constantly has renewed its strength.

Together with a friend, I have reworked the original text and made some short additions. Published in this book also is an excellent and very practical introduction to the Jesus Prayer written by a monk from the Eastern Church.

The Jesus Prayer is the fruit of a long tradition. It has been developed from the reverence for God's name in the Bible, and especially the use of Jesus' name in the New Testament, via the Desert Fathers' prayer methods, to the spiritual movement in the Eastern Church which began during the fifth century and goes by the name of hesykasmen [hesychia]. The emphasis in this tradition is laid on deep inner prayer. "Hesychia" means the soul's repose.

The Hesychast movement bloomed at Mount Athos and later made its way to Russia where the Jesus Prayer put down deep roots in the broad strata of the people. Its definitive formulation was in *The Philokalia*.[1] The Jesus Prayer's popularity was renewed at the end of the nineteenth century through the publication of *A Russian Pilgrim's Tales*,[2] and at last reached the West.

This modest little piece proceeds from the question: what can the Jesus Prayer teach us about Christian prayer in general? One doesn't need to look far in order to discover that the fundamental features in the Eastern and Western prayer traditions have considerable similarity. Therefore, it seems completely clear to me that the deep prayer life is the most direct way to Christian unity.

Since this above all is a matter of the Jesus Prayer's innermost core and its universal meaning in the prayer's world, I do not limit myself only to the specifically hesykast sources. The Desert Fathers do not speak directly about the Jesus Prayer but its essence and spirit are everywhere present among them.

On Praying the Name of Jesus

The simple surrender to Jesus' name and person, where all else is forsaken in order to make way for him alone, is also deeply interlaced with my own Carmelite tradition. Little Thérèse (of Lisieux), with her teaching about *happiness* in being a sinner, totally dependent on Jesus' compassion and merciful love, provides the synthesis in the piece. One could say that she is herself the personified and incarnate Jesus Prayer.

"I know that if the unlikely should happen that you found a weaker and more insignificant soul than mine, you would shower them with even greater gifts of grace if she, with complete trust, gave herself over to your endless mercy. But why even want to announce your secrets of love, Jesus? It is you alone who have taught them to me and you can just as well reveal them to others."[3]

WILFRID STINISSEN

1

The Tradition of the Desert Fathers

The Jesus Prayer receives its first definitive formulation in the hesykasmen. Nevertheless, one cannot deny that it has its origin in the tradition of the Desert Fathers. We know that these Fathers customarily repeated short prayers out of the Bible. According to Augustine they shot these prayers like arrows up to God, hence one speaks of "shot-prayers." One of their most esteemed prayers was this invocation: "Be pleased, O God, to deliver me. O Lord, make haste to help me!" (Psalm 70:1).

Through this constant repetition of God's word, they could recognize themselves in the words of the psalmist: "Oh, how I love your law! It is my meditation all day long" (Ps 119:97). The words "ponder" or "meditate" indicate in the Bible to slowly and lovingly repeat the law's word.

In the study of different testimony about the formulations of prayers used by the Fathers, it is surprising that already one could find all of the elements of the

Jesus Prayer. So is the respect for The Name apparent in this saying: "When you hear reports of the holy father's elevated way of life, try then to follow after them and invoke the Name of the Lord."[4] Abba Ammonas advises us to repeat this prayer: "Be merciful to me a sinner: Have always the word of the publican in your heart, then you can be saved."[5] Abba Makarios replies to the question as to how one should pray, in this way: "One does not need to be verbose, but it's enough to extend your hands and say: 'Lord, according to your will and your wisdom, show mercy.'"[6]

In spite of the fact that the Fathers do not speak expressly about breathing, one can wonder if the sighs which according to them follow the prayers are not the first stage in the development which in the seventh century leads to Johannes Klimakos' known rule: "Let the remembrance of Jesus be united with your breathing."[7]

The most striking thing in the aphorisms of the Desert Fathers is without a doubt the contribution of the heart. This "penthos"—pain caused by my own or others' sins—has prepared the soil so that the Jesus Prayer can come to flower there. Life in the desert was favorable for this inner look and made it clear and piercing.

The fight against the devil, and above all against the devil in one's own heart, brought all the hidden remnants of pride and selfishness into the light of day. Can one do anything but weep when sin in this way is revealed in all its horrible depth? When Abba Pastor got to see a woman who was crying bitterly at a grave, he said: "Even if all the world's losses were given to her, they couldn't draw up her soul from this *penthos*. In the same way, the monk must always have this *penthos*."[8]

It is typical for the Desert Fathers that they in contrast to the hesykasts are very inventive, when they speak about temptations and thoughts (*logismoi*). While the hesykasts, with unfailing trust, praise the Jesus Prayer as an unfailing medicine against the devil's attack, the Desert Fathers have several different methods which are adapted to life's shifting vicissitudes. One can divide these methods into two categories: methods where one directly battles against temptation and methods where one doesn't bother about temptation, but immediately raises his heart to God.

Evagrios (c. 345–399) is a representative of the first category. Instead of ignoring the evil thoughts, which means a risk of suppressing them, and immediately exchanging them for thoughts about God, according to Evagrios one should instead let these thoughts come up to the level of clear consciousness. As soon as the evil thoughts become completely conscious, one can begin to struggle and go to a direct attack against them by an opposed thought. In this way, someone who has been beset by a thought which has something to do with greed and at the same time feels himself inclined to deny a suffering brother his charity, first accepts this temptation and so to say looks it right in the face. Thereafter he has to destroy it with these words from the Book of Deuteronomy: "Do not be hard-hearted or tight-fisted toward your needy neighbor. You should rather open your hand" (Deut 15:7–8).[9] Abba Antonius advises us quite simply to receive the thoughts and accept them. If it appears that any of them are dangerous, one should attach them with a word from Scripture: "He humbled you by letting you hunger, then by feeding you with manna, with which neither you nor your ancestors were acquainted, in order to make you understand that one does not live by bread alone, but by every word that comes from the mouth of the Lord" (Deut 8:3).

When hunger says to you: "Drink a little wine, like the blessed Timothy," reply thus: "Remember the child of Jonabab who obeyed his father's prohibition" (Jer 35:6). When sleep threatens to overcome you, don't give in, for in the holy Gospel it is written: "Stay awake and pray" (Mt 26:41). It is also written: "The stout-hearted were stripped of their spoil; they sank into sleep" (Ps 76:5). Feed your soul with God's word, with wakefulness and prayer, and above all with the unceasing remembrance of our Lord Jesus Christ's name. In this way you will find the way to conquer the evil thoughts.[10]

Other Fathers discovered that one can cheat temptations by apparently giving in to them. It is told about Abba Theodoros and Abba Lukios that they were beset by the temptation to leave their hermitage. They let this thought go and said: "After winter is over we will go." When it then became summer, they said: "When summer is past, we will go." And so it continued season after season for fifty years.[11] A little psychological trick like this shows great wisdom of life.

All temptations threaten to degenerate into obsessions. In such cases, the Fathers don't hesitate to play a little theater, which gives them the possibility of easing the all-too-great tensions. A brother is badly pained by the temptation to visit an old monk. Day after day, he pushed the forbidden thought away. For three years, he fought in this way against the temptation. Finally, he said to himself: "Assume that you have come to the old man and say to him: 'How are you, my father? I have for a long time longed to see your holiness.' Then he took a washtub, bathed, and play the role of the old monk: 'It is good that you have come here, my brother. Excuse me, you have gone to a lot of trouble for my sake. May the Lord reward you for that.' Thereafter he took his meal, ate, and drank to his heart's content and immediately the temptation was gone." [12]

Psychodrama is no discovery of our own time! The Desert Fathers show evidence of a surprisingly deep psychological insight. They know full well that no one can find the truth about God if they reject the truth about themselves. Sometimes they maintain the proposition that, in order to know God, we first must learn to know ourselves. Sometimes they emphasize that the deeper knowledge about God which prayer provides casts new light over the praying man's inner condition. The most important thing is never, of your own free will, shut your eyes to this growing self-knowledge. Some Fathers go still farther and advise that during the course of the prayer pray-ers examine their lives or analyze distractions, to try to find out their origins. Instead of rejecting distractions or suppressing them, one turns consciously to them in order to make a careful analysis. This direct confrontation is not seldom seen as a necessary preparation for the contact with God. Without self-knowledge the relation with God risks remaining a little hesitant and not having any influence on daily life.

From the foregoing one still cannot draw the conclusion that it is always necessary to deal with thoughts and temptations in an active way. The Fathers say also that we should directly turn to God. Makarios gives a monk the following advice: "If a thought arises in you, don't look downward but always upwards, then the Lord will come immediately to your help."[13] Abba Johannes says: "I resemble a man who sits under a large tree and who sees how many wild beasts and snakes come towards him. When he understands that he cannot escape them, he climbs quickly up the tree and is saved. So it is with me: I sit in my cell and observe how the evil thoughts come against me, and when I cannot resist them, I flee to God in prayer and am saved from the enemy."[14]

It is apparent that the Jesus Prayer belongs to this second category. Instead of directly fighting against the temptations, one finds refuge in Jesus' name. This way of turning oneself directly to God is, without doubt, often the shortest and quickest way. No one has described its advantages more convincingly than Saint John of the Cross. In connection with the "anagogic"—upward climbing—act, he says: "When we discover an initial enticement, or an attack from some vice, such as unchastity, rage, impatience, or vindictiveness because of some wrong we have had to suffer, we should immediately, when we experience this, make some movement of anagogic love, while we lift our hearts up to a union with God. By raising itself upwards in this way, the soul escapes and steps forth before God, with whom it unites, and in this way the intentions of the vice and the temptation and the enemy are shamed, and they find no one they can damage. For the soul, which is more evident when it loves or when it gives life, has in a divine way jerked back the body from temptation, and so the enemy finds nowhere to strike a blow or entangle, since the soul no longer is where the temptation or the enemy will wound and damage it. And then, something wonderful happens! It is as if the soul had forgotten the enticements of vice, it has united with and become one with its Beloved and feels no enticement at all from the vice through which the devil will tempt it. It has succeeded with this, because—as we said—it jerked the body away and it was no longer there. It is, thus, almost like tempting a dead body, if one can say this, or like fighting something which isn't there, something which feels nothing and which therefore cannot be tempted." [15] Can't we say that the invocation of Jesus' name is the best example of an anagogic act?

But Saint John of the Cross is conscious that, in many situations, above all for neophytes (and how many ever leave this stage completely?), it's not enough with anagogic acts. According to Father Eliseus of the Martyrs: "One must warn novices, whose loving or anagogic acts are not so quick, easy, or burning, against believing that with one single leap they can distance themselves completely and be united with the Bridegroom, and that they, if they are to see that through such an anagogic act and movement, cannot totally forget temptation's sinful allure, and they should not omit to draw profit from all the weapons and thoughts they can find in order to make resistance until they have completely conquered the temptation."[16]

For Saint John of the Cross the anagogic act is a more perfect way than the direct struggle where one employs the opposing virtue (or thinks the "opposing thoughts" that Evagrios talks about). Not everyone seems to be in agreement on this. So thinks, for example, John the Prophet (5th–6th centuries) who, together with Barsanufios is one of the most attractive representatives of the Eastern Church's monastic tradition, that the anagogic act is especially suited for the weak.

A monk posed of him the question as to how he would combat an evil thought: "Through direct attack—or through flight to God and placing one's powerlessness before him?" John replied to him: "Whatever evil enticement we are exposed to, we can do no better than to invoke God's name. As to the direct attack, it isn't suitable for each and every one but only for someone who is powerful in the eyes of God and to whom the devils submit—But we who are weak beings can do no more than to take refuge in Jesus' name."[17] The opposition between these two saints undoubtedly only seems so: "The weak beings" that John the Prophet speaks about are far from novices but the kind of persons who have accepted their weakness and just because of this, thanks to their humility, don't need to be pushed into the background in any way by the "powerful in God's eyes."

Perhaps it is to some degree regrettable that hesykasm has concentrated so much and exclusively on the Jesus Prayer that all other methods of prayer have been put in the shade. The hesykasts have perhaps not to a sufficiently high degree seen that the Jesus Prayer, in certain situations, can be a flight or suppression attempt. Doesn't Jesus say that one must leave his gift before the altar and be reconciled to his brother and sister? (Mt 5:24). In the same way it can also be useful, even necessary, to first look certain "thoughts" in the eye and expressly deal with them. Through a radicalism which is perhaps exaggerated, hesykasm has at least partially lost its psychological and spiritual experience which the Desert Fathers in their wisdom had assembled.

$$\overline{2}$$

The Formulation of
the Jesus Prayer

The Jesus Prayer has been called "a synthesis of all theology." Even if this contention can seem pointed, nevertheless we have to admit that this prayer has great riches. It expresses man's basic attitudes toward God. God wants to save human beings. The human must let himself be saved. He opens himself to salvation by acknowledging that he is a sinner.

The first part of the prayer, "Lord Jesus Christ, Son of God," is a confession of faith. We confirm that Jesus is Christ, that is to say, the Messiah, the anointed one. "Jesus is nothing if he is not Christ, and Christ is nothing if he is not Jesus."[18] Jesus is also God's Son, light of light, true God of true God. It is in the divine nature of Christ that the foundation of our unlimited trust is to be found. That Jesus has been sent by the Father to save us and is also himself God, "of the same being as the Father," is the bedrock on which we can build our house (cf. Mt 7:24). One cannot repeat these words without, at the same time, growing in bold trust.

Jesus' greatness stands in contrast to the insignificance of humans. This is expressed in the second part of the prayer: "have mercy on me, a sinner." You are everything, I am nothing. Instead of camouflaging the sin or suppressing it, we admit it honestly. "If we confess our sins, he who is faithful and just will forgive us our sins and cleanse us from all unrighteousness" (1 Jn 1:9). The real prayers always stream up "out of the depths" (Ps 120:1). In order to attain the All, one must first sink down into nothingness. "And I descended so low, so low that I climbed so high, so high, that I caught up with the exchange."[19]

The Jesus Prayer's formulation is not an absolute thing, but to constantly change it is certainly not to be recommended. On the other hand, a certain inventiveness can contribute to greater consciousness. Thus one can instead of using the long formulation, pray like the Russian pilgrim: "Lord Jesus Christ, have mercy on me." One can even simplify the formulation to just the name "Jesus."

Some will perhaps think that his way of repeating the name of Jesus is suspect, like transcendental meditation. This consists, as is well known, in the incessant of a mantra one has received at an initiation ceremony. There is, however, a deep and fundamental difference: The mantra is a sound without meaning which is mechanically repeated, but in the Jesus Prayer, on the other hand, one "prays" the name attentively and respectfully. The name is a sacrament for a loving presence. The name signifies the whole person and becomes meaningful only when we know the one who bears it. At the same time, the name becomes—when it is allowed to have its full significance—a gateway to a deeper and deeper encounter with this person's mystery.

Transcendentalism's mantra can anchor us in ourselves. To express the name of the Beloved—express it with love—on the other hand, creates a *relation*.

The Jesus Prayer can easily be fitted to liturgical times and holidays. During the Christmas season, one can, for example, pray: "Lord Jesus Christ, who became man for me, have mercy on me." During Easter, "Lord Jesus Christ, who arose for me, have mercy on me." At the feast of the Transfiguration: "Lord Jesus Christ, who became glorified on the mountain...." With variations, the prayer becomes an extension of the liturgy, it becomes a little liturgy which is in harmony with the Church's great liturgy.

The Eastern tradition does not recognize any narrow delimitation between liturgical and private prayers. The recitation of the Jesus Prayer can even replace the liturgical prayers in accord with a table, which specifies the prescribed number.[20]

In certain orthodox abbeys, this takes place at the community level: a large part of the scheduled acts consist in silently listening to the Jesus Prayer, which is prayed aloud by one of the monks or nuns.

There is also a place for Mary in the Jesus Prayer. The holy Maximos, a monk on Mount Athos during the fourteenth century, beseeched Mary with tears to grant him the grace of prayer. "When he stood before the icon of the Virgin Mary, he experienced a sweet warmth in his breast; whereupon his heart began to express the prayer. Maximos united the remembrance of Jesus with the remembrance of the Mother of God."[21] Is it not Mary's job to wake Jesus to life in us, and consequently also the Jesus Prayer? The holy Serafim of Sarov (1759–1833) recommends a Marian version of the Jesus Prayer, especially for the afternoon hours: "Lord Jesus Christ, Son of God, have mercy on me, a sinner, through the intercession of the Mother of God."

For many, the Jesus Prayer is a quick way to composure, peace, and harmony. The slow, rhythmic repetition leads to a more intense concentration and attention to greater simplicity and unity, to deeper peace. But that's not all. In a certain sense, the Jesus Prayer is also at the end of the road. Because holiness consists in union with Jesus, one can say that the Jesus Prayer is a growing holiness. Every time you utter the name of Jesus, you forget yourself and let yourself become lost in him. Every time your self dies, it causes you to live more for Jesus. It is a movement away from the superficial ego toward your center which is the living presence of Jesus in you. The more you are fortified and rooted there, the more you become transformed, made divine. You can say, with Saint Paul: "It is no longer I who live, but it is Christ who lives in me" (Gal 2:20).

3

The Heart's Prayer

The Jesus Prayer is also called the heart's prayer. Actually, each prayer ought to be, or become, a prayer from the heart. That this is especially true for the Jesus Prayer is dependent on the heart receiving a special place.

Let us, in the first place, note that "the heart" in this sense does not have the same meaning as in contemporary speech. It has nothing to do with external feelings. In this tradition of the Eastern Church which goes back to the Bible, the heart is the human being's most important organ, both from a physical and a spiritual point of view. It is also the place where the human being has contact with God. It is there, in the depths of the human heart, that the divine life slumbers.

In the *Catechism of the Catholic Church*, it says: "The heart is the place where I maintain myself, where I live (according to the Semitic or biblical way of speaking, the place to which 'I descend'). The heart is our hidden core, incomprehensible to our understanding, or to other men. Only God's Spirit can find this out and know it. The heart is the deepest foundation of the psychic life, where men make their basic decision. It is the place of truth, where we choose between life and death. It is a meeting place, since we, in the image of God, live in relation to each other: The heart is the place of the uniting covenant."[22]

In paradise man lived in his heart. He was in harmony with God and there was a complete accord between his intellect and his feelings. The result of the Fall is that the unity in man's nature was broken up and torn apart. He has lost his center and the result is that he is now drowning in superficial things. The harmony of paradise, which was given to us and for which we were created, has become lost. Thoughts, images, desires, and feelings now fight against one another and it is difficult for us to turn the whole of our being toward God. Even if the soul in its depths has a painful yearning for him, the surface is teeming with smaller and larger cravings which constantly say "no." This split has its seat in the head, where thoughts and images "whirl around like snowflakes or swarms of mosquitoes in the summer" (Theofan Eremitan, 1815–1894).

The orthodox anthropology strongly emphasizes this split between head and heart in fallen man. Sin creates chaos. The unity and harmony which prevailed between the heart—the capital possession by which we are enabled to know and experience God—and the head—the rational and sensual or perceptive knowledge of the external world—is broken. The person's integrity, his wholeness, consists just in a harmonious relation between these two poles, where understanding submits to the heart. It is only by living more deeply in this truth about ourselves and by bearing this truth to God that we can attain unity within ourselves.

For this reason the spiritual writers of the Eastern Church repeat constantly anew that in prayer, it is important to leave the head and sink down into the heart. This is not only a spiritual process. By the term "heart" is meant also the physical organ which has a determined place in our body, "near the left nipple, a bit above it," as Ignatius Brianchaninov (1807–1867) says.[23] The body's heart is in itself a symbol for the spiritual heart. Therefore the search for the heart has both a physical and a spiritual aspect. To listen to the beating heart makes it easier to find our spiritual center. But the whole body can help us to this if we try to be consciously present in it and convey it to God by not getting caught up in our tensions. "My heart and my flesh sing for joy to the living God" (Ps 84:2).

One should be able to believe that this sinking down in the heart is a natural consequence of the monotonous repetition of the Jesus Prayer. In this case, it would be best to think as little as possible about the content of the formulation and be satisfied with a mechanical repetition which automatically attains the desired result. But, as we have already mentioned, the Fathers are—on the contrary—agreed that one should devote one's full attention to the meaning of the words. What it concerns is not leaving one's understanding behind in the head but to leave it sink down in the heart together with the word. It is just through this attention that harmony between head and heart is restored.

We can distinguish three degrees in the development of prayer. In the beginning, it is often a prayer with the lips. While the tongue repeats the words, the thoughts continue to swarm around.

When you succeed in reaching the content of the words, you have reached the second degree—the prayer of understanding. Here you reach already a first form of unity: Through the constant conscious repetition of the same word, the thoughts cease their travels and the understanding concentrates on the meaning of the words. Afterwards, as you rise up to this meaning with your whole essence and not only with your understanding, and at the same time during the prayer look for the place of the heart, it can happen that eventually you experience how the prayer sinks down into the heart. This is the third degree.

§ This sinking down should actually be experienced in the literal way: it is a question of both physical and spiritual movement from the head down toward the heart. Some are able already on their first attempt to experience something of this.

To a certain degree, the entire spiritual development, especially for us Westerners, deals with this transfer from the head to the heart. The turning away from God has caused us to move our center to the intellect where we think we have a grip on the environment and can steer and manage things ourselves. We become more deserted in the heart and dependent because we there meet a reality which is larger than our conception. There awakens the need to turn toward something else. It is a great gift to know this "something by name."

When the understanding has found its way back to its area of origin, it will gladly return there. It will of course not immediately liberate itself from the bad habits of rushing around in the inner desert which an exclusively intellectual knowledge amounts to. But it knows, in any event, a growing homesickness for the heart which it has recognized as its true home. What was in the beginning in each case a cold and dry understanding allows itself to be more and more leavened by the wisdom of the heart. It becomes equipped with spiritual sense and gets a sensitive understanding of divine things. But the heart becomes also richer when the understanding assumes its right place; it becomes a serene and understanding heart.

However, it is not enough only to step into your heart. The heart has a limitless space into which we constantly can penetrate more deeply. The Jesus Prayer can be compared with a drilling machine. It drills through all our psyche's stony and barren layers in a search for the water which is found in the depths. Because this water is the living water that Jesus talks about (Jn 4:10), the life of the Spirit, which in its essence is limitless, comes looking at full speed only when we have found what we have been seeking. When one sinks down into the heart, one never reaches the limit. "I know that in this bottomless river no one has waded toward a beach and reached it."[24]

4

A Prayer Which Concerns Both Soul and Body

The Jesus Prayer is a clear example of prayer which also concerns the body. It is not only the prayer of the soul but of the whole person. And it is the whole person that is transformed through it. The Eastern Church more than we in the West has remained faithful to the Semitic and biblical view of humankind. When an old wise man wants to teach the Russian pilgrim the unceasing prayer, he looks in *The Philokalia*, and reads a piece from Simeon the New Theologian (949–1022 A.D.): "Sit down, quietly and alone, bow your head, shut year eyes, breathe slowly and look with the powers of your imagination into your heart, and lead your reason, that is, your thoughts from the head to the heart. With each breath, you should say: 'Lord Jesus Christ, have mercy on me!' You should express the words slowly and quietly, with the lips or only with the breath."[25]

Even when we are bothered by distracting thoughts, the body can help us to come more easily and quickly to an inner composure. "If you, in spite of your efforts, cannot penetrate the land of the heart, as you have been shown, do then what I say to you and with God's help you will find what you are seeking. You know that the power to bring forth words is to be found in each person's thought. Use this power, chase away all other thoughts (you can if you want to) and let it constantly repeat these words: 'Lord Jesus Christ, have mercy on me!' Force yourself to constantly repeat anew the words of the prayer. If you for some time keep this up, the entry to your heart will surely be open for your prayer. This has been taught by experience."[26]

Many other Fathers and spiritual authors give the advice to pray the Jesus Prayer in time with your breathing. At the intake: "Lord Jesus (Christ)." At the out take: "have mercy on me." Or: "Lord" on the intake, "Jesus" on the out take; "have mercy" on the intake, "on me" on the out take. The interplay between the breathing and the words makes the Jesus Prayer afterwards seem as natural as the act of breathing itself. The time will come when the one will draw the other with it.

The Jesuit, Father Franz Jalics, who conducts a retreat house in Germany, prescribes a repetition of "Jesus" when breathing out and "Christ" when breathing in. This form can be seen almost a bit backward in the beginning. But just because of the fact that in the pause after breathing out we expect to have a completed prayer by saying "Christ," there is created a composure and perseverance.[27]

It is, however, not absolutely necessary to pray the Jesus Prayer in time with breathing. Lively discussions about this have taken place over the course of history. Theofan the Hermit writes: "It is important—to some degree—to have the breathing under control so that you can fit it to the rhythm of the words."[28]

On the other hand, he is strict toward those who place great weight on the breathing techniques, recommending this or that Father. He advises against this even if he admits at the same time that he can be caught up by this himself: "We give our dear brothers not to try this method if it doesn't spontaneously begin to work in them. Among those who have tried them out, there are a number who have caused injury to the lungs without accomplishing anything. The mechanical methods which are described in this work can with good result be replaced by slower repetition of the prayer, with a short pause after each invocation, with a calm and slow catching of the breath, and a striving to keep the understanding caught in the words of the prayer. With the help of the means, one can without toil make headway and even attentiveness grows. After a short time, the heart begins to live 'in tune' with the praying intellect. Eventually this develops into the unity of the heart and the intellect, and then the methods recommended by the Fathers begin to work of their own accord."[29]

Personally I think that one who has learned to live in his body does not at all experience the psychophysical method as something "mechanical." It is the body's natural participation in the prayers, and it gives them a special richness and completeness. On the other hand, if the body is a stranger rather than a friend, the method must at least in the beginning act as a hindrance. It is also clear that Theofan's warning is above all directed at those who would devote their entire lives to the Jesus Prayer. For those who would only spend twenty minutes or a half hour each day, there is scarcely any risk.

The hands can also be a help in reaching deeper into the prayer of the heart. Franz Jalics teaches his readers and retreat participants to hold their hands together so that the palms rest against each other. In the middle of the palm there is a sensitive nerve center and when both hands meet there, relaxed without pressing together, it is easy to experience the current of life. This brings about a special nearness to him who is the source of life.

One cannot treat the role of the body in the Jesus Prayer without mentioning what many Fathers call the "baptism of tears." The tears unite the body with the soul, they express the harmony between the inner and the outer person. When the person weeps, he is expressing his heart's contrition, and, at the same time, his thanks for God's forgiving and renewing love. In fact, it can be difficult to distinguish between crying for one's sins or for God's goodness. It is, rather, a "painful joy"[30] which through these tears becomes visible. Someone I know says that there is a noticeable difference between this "spiritual" weeping, which breaks forth through a deep inner encounter with God, and the purely "earthly" weeping which comes from our sorrows in this world, and which naturally also has its justification. The "spiritual" weeping creates calm and composure, it never distresses.

The tears bring about a catharsis in the soul. It is a bath of spiritual and psychic rebirth. The prayers should not be sentimental. But over many centuries one has nevertheless prayed in the Roman liturgy about the gift of the tears. Why should we hide and suppress our real feelings? If your prayer is dry and naysaying, it can result in our emotional life having shriveled up. Those who live in their superficial feelings never find God. But those who are anchored in their depths can let the tears flow without losing anything of their confidence. Those who cry like this are blessed.

$$\frac{}{5}$$

Unceasing Prayer

The advice to pray the Jesus Prayer sitting, immobile, with closed eyes, does not mean at all that this prayer should be reserved for special places and times. One can pray it on the street, while one is getting dressed, in the kitchen, in the evening before going to sleep. Many have had the experience that on a bus or train, the prayer is bound up with a special grace. "Don't neglect at making an inner prayer when you sit on the train on Friday. I know myself that one has then an exceptional opportunity,"[31] wrote Sister Elizabeth of the Trinity from the Carmelite Cloister to her mother. All the empty moments of the day— and those who begin to be attentive about this matter note that in retrospect they have grown in frequency— one can fill with the Jesus Prayer.

Not only empty moments, since this prayer is so utterly simple and uncomplicated one can even pray it during many apparently "filled" moments. As long as our work doesn't demand our complete attention we can let it be permeated with prayer.

A word which is performed with Jesus, enveloped in his loving presence, cannot be anything but blessed.

By often praying the Jesus Prayer, there grows a new disposition toward nature and creation. In a beautiful text, the Russian pilgrim bears witness to this inner transformation: "When I began to pray in the heart, everything about me appeared in a wonderful form— the trees, the grass, birds, earth, air, light—everything seemed to say to me that it was created for man as a sign of God's love for him. Everything prayed to God, everything worshiped him. I saw now what was meant by 'to understand what the creation says' and I saw how it could be possible to converse with God's created beings."[32]

Just as everything was created in the Word (cf. Jn 1:3), there is nothing which doesn't bear his stamp. Everything which exists has a part of the Son's sending: to reveal the Father (Jn 1:18). The whole universe proclaims God's glory. But this song of praise is like music on notepaper, which awaits an artist who can awaken it to life. Man has received the wonderful power to interpret the cosmic music. Without him it remains mute.

The people of Israel knew this; they never ceased to invite the entire creation to songs of praise and jubilation: "Make a joyful noise to God, all the earth; sing the glory of his name" (Ps 66:1–2).

Humans are only in harmony with creation when they carry out their priestly role, and by this, offer creation to God. Instead of looking down upon creation or violating it, they accord to it a deep worth. They lead it to the goal for which it was created and perceive that it should not be rejected but glorified and transformed. Things bother humans as long as they have not discovered the mark of God in them. Indeed, the world becomes a source of suffering and trouble if one does not see that it is a monstrance, "God's tabernacle among men" (Rev 21:3).

Because the invocation of the name binds us to the person of Jesus, it binds us also with others. When the Word became flesh and assumed a human nature, it integrated at the same time all of humanity in itself. We are all the members of the Body of Christ (1 Cor 6:15). By more and more incorporating ourselves in him, we become more attached to others. When you have discovered that Jesus dwells in your heart (Eph 3:17), you can only find him in the hearts of others. While you repeat the name of Jesus, you repeat the true names of your brothers and sisters.

Jesus fulfills each and every one of us. He is the most personal in each person. You see the other as the Father sees him, he who in each person recognizes his Son in whom he has his happiness. Each face becomes an icon. You agree easily with the Patriarch Athenagoras (1886–1972): "The face is a miracle. What happiness it is to dive down into the eyes of the other, in the inner ocean of his eyes."[33]

The Russian pilgrim is also pleasantly surprised by this new love and happiness: "When during the day I met people by chance I thought that they all showed such goodness—to invoke the name of Jesus was enough to give me happiness on my way. All persons showed me goodness. It was as if all of them loved me."[34]

The Song of Solomon says that the name of the Beloved is "an anointing oil" (Song 1:3). With this oil we can anoint everyone we meet by speaking the name of Jesus over them. Thanks to the sharp eye which is the fruit of prayer, we can more quickly feel what suffering the other person is bearing. Why not then try to heal this suffering by anointing the wounds with the balsam of the holy name? This spiritual anointing can be a way of expressing a longing that the other person will finally discover his deepest essence. We want him to experience the sweetness and fragrance which is found in the name of Jesus, which also has its own innermost name.

Often the prayer goes from the singular: "Have mercy on me" imperceptibly over into the plural form: "Have mercy on us." Jesus' words—"You are all brothers"

(Mt 23:8)—acquires a new meaning. To each and every one we want to say: "You are my flesh and blood!" (Gen 29:14). By invoking the name and praying for mercy "over us," there is born a true community and the Church is built up, not directly on the outer plane, but on this "radical" plane, that is, on a level which takes the roots (radix) themselves to the visible, institutional, and sacramental plane. For this reason, the Jesus Prayer has an ecumenical scope whose consequences cannot be reckoned or foreseen. By creating unity among Christians, it prepares also for the unity of the Church.

The Church is a community of saints and sinners, the field where weeds and wheat grow together (cf. Mt 13:24–30). The Jesus Prayer with its two poles, "Jesus Christ" and "me, a sinner," strengthens this double community. Solidarity in belonging to Christ does not in any way exclude solidarity at the level of sin. Those who have been freed by Christ necessarily discover the deep darkness of sin. The first question which the old Russian *starets* Sophrony (1896–1992)—himself a disciple to the holy *starets* Silvan (1866–1938)—posed, when I visited with two fellow brothers, his cloister in England, was this: "Have you found moments in your life when you felt yourself far distant from God?" He had tears in his eyes when he asked us this. When we replied in the affirmative he seemed to be relieved. This little overture caused us from the beginning to have a feeling of deep solidarity and being placed in an atmosphere of prayer.

Only when we get to know that God's purity is constantly raised over our baseness, and suffer from this, can we find him in a new way. The pain derived from the distance between God and ourselves is at the same time a joy—if we dare accept and confess our lack of purity. Our incapacity to receive more of God's gifts. Our sin digs out a depth within us which cries out and implores that we be filled with God's depth. The deep cries out to the deep (Ps 42:7).

When you know that you yourself are a sinner among sinners, you have no need to criticize and judge others. "He who recognizes his own stench in his nose cannot recognize any other smell even if he stands on a pile with dead bodies," said Barsanufios (d. circa 540) in a somewhat drastic way.[35] Instead of praying for the "poor sinners," you will pray now for "us sinners." You no longer see any obvious lines between your own sin and that of others. In confession, you no longer acknowledge only your "individual" sins, if the word now has any meaning in this connection. You carry the sins of the entire world and know that you are responsible for them. Like little Thérèse, you sit down at the table with sinners, not as their benefactor but as the "most wretched of them all."[36]

6

Tranquility and Temperance

The story about the Russian pilgrim gives some impression that the Jesus Prayer must be prayed constantly. A *starets* challenges the pilgrim in the beginning to pray the prayer three thousand time, then six thousand times, then, finally, twelve thousand times a day.[37] The goal of this intensive training is that the prayer should be so at one with the heart that the heart begins eventually to pray the prayer in time with its own pulse rate. When this stage has been reached, the words no longer need to be repeated actively. It is enough to listen carefully to the heart which has now become a living prayer.

Apart from someone who has received a special calling, confirmed by an experienced spiritual director, I don't think that it is wise to embark on such a radical path. First and foremost, it is difficult to find the time to do this. Not even someone in a contemplative cloister finds it possible to repeat the Jesus Prayer twelve thousand times a day. And one cannot hope to integrate the Jesus Prayer with the heart's beat if one has not prayed it over a longer time pretty constantly. Even among the hermits on Mount Athos, it is difficult to find someone who has come so far. One can also pose the question whether Western man has sufficient psychic iron to dare to take the path. Furthermore, there is only a disappearing small possibility to find an experienced *starets.*

Fortunately, the orthodox tradition recognizes another direction which is represented by, among others, the Archimandrite Sophrony. When I asked him if it was desirable to follow the example of the Russian pilgrim and constantly repeat the Jesus Prayer, he replied that this prayer, on the contrary, should be seen as a point of departure, a springboard into tranquility. He thought that it sometimes was enough to utter the Jesus Prayer one time in order to rest in the prayer later. When distracting thoughts arise anew, one takes refuge again in the words of the prayer.

The monk from the Eastern Church who wrote the first part of this book writes: "The Name pronounced may be extended and prolonged in seconds or minutes of silent rest and attention. The repetition of the Name may be likened to the beating of wings by which a bird rises into the air...."[38]

Theofan the Hermit says something similar: "The third degree is the prayer of experience. Thanks to our inner composure the heart has warmed up so that what hitherto was no more than a thought now becomes experience. While in the beginning it was only a formulation for repentance, now it develops into repentance itself, and what in the beginning was no more than a question expressed in words is transformed now into an experience of radical need. Those who have passed through the stages of action and real experience pray without words, for God is the heart's God." [39] The holy Serafim of Sarov gives Motovilov the advice to pray until God makes himself known, "When one is visited by him, one must stop and pray [he means: to use words]. Why should one call out to him and say: 'Come and to us, cleanse us from every detriment and save our soul, you who are Goodness itself' [orthodox troparion], if he has already found himself in us as a reply to our humble and loving prayer?" [40]

For these writers, the Jesus Prayer is a road to tranquility. If we have attained this tranquility, the calling out is an obstacle. One is reminded of the famous picture of the stairs in Saint John of the Cross: "If those who climb up the stairs don't leave them after themselves, the one after the other all the way to the very last one, but will stay on one of them, so they will never come up, they will never reach the pleasant and peaceful room that is the goal. It is the same way with the soul which already in this life will attain union with him who is our highest rest and our highest good. Step by step, they must pass all the different outlooks, conceptions, and degrees of knowledge, and leave them behind, for they have nothing in common with or proportion to the goals which they lead to, that is to say, God."[41]

Jesus says to the disciples: "It is to your advantage that I go away" (Jn 16:7). When he is no longer visibly present, he can announce a deeper, entirely spiritual presence. In the same way, it is good that the words "to leave us" during the prayer leads to making way for tranquility. Silence opens new doors within us where words can never reach. Words are important and unavoidable, but they can only fulfill their right function when we recognize their limits and know that they should be less in order that silence be greater (cf. Jn 3:30).

There is another kind of tranquility to which the Orthodox tradition attaches great weight and refers to as "näphis" (from "näphô," to refrain from wine). This expression means both abstemiousness and vigilance, two inner attitudes which Paul already placed side by side: "Let us keep awake and be sober" (1 Thess 5:6). Those who become intoxicated lose control over the power of their souls, but the sober, restrained man can, on the other hand, "look after" his thoughts and feelings. According to hesykasmen, restraint and watchfulness lead the way for inner tranquility, which is the basic condition for all prayers.

Restraint demands that during prayer one turn away every thought and every inner conception. The prayer is more pure the more destitute it is. Of course, the Orthodox Church has its icons which play an important part in the liturgy and in the personal life of the believer. Nevertheless, one should be able to maintain that not even here is lacking restraint. The icon is never naturalistic, it never has the ambition to be an exact copy of reality, but it seeks through its timeless character to express something of the unspeakable. The inner prayer demands, however, an even greater restraint. It means a confrontation in the middle of the desert, between two realities which cannot be captured in words: Christ the Savior's love and sinful man's misery. This meeting has to take place in a direct, even abrupt way. If it would be mediated through a third party it would lose the greater part of its liberating power.

The demand for total destitution is also found with the one who is called the "master-teacher of the mystical night." The following text shows what he thinks about this: "Therefore, O spiritual soul, you should free yourself from the dust, all the small hairs, and the fog and make your eye clean. If you do so the sun will illuminate you and you will see clearly. Continue your soul in peace, take it away from and make it free from the yoke and the slavery which its own weak activity and capability inflict on it, which is like the captivity in Egypt, where there was nothing to do but collect straw and make bricks (Ex 1:14). And you, spiritual director, you should lead it to the promised land flowing with milk and honey."[42]

The only, certainly very important, difference is that Saint John of the Cross only demands this total destitution of the soul which God has already set into a condition of contemplation and thus in itself has recognized the so-called three signs. The Orthodox writers seem here to give proof of great daring. According to them, one can and must reject all images as soon as one begins to employ the Jesus Prayer. Of course, this negative disposition holds only during the prayer time itself.

But the thoughts and images incessantly march by the door of the heart and seek to force it. What is one to do? According to the Fathers, one ought to set out a guard post for the heart, not just during prayer but for the whole day. This is another aspect of the concept "näphis" which here, above all else, means watchfulness. Every time a thought strikes, you meet it with the name of Jesus which you invoke in your heart. If the thought is good, it will survive this encounter, step into the heart, put down roots and afterwards bear fruit. An evil thought, on the other hand, is crushed against the name of Jesus. The Scriptures tell about Jefta and Gilead's men who forced the fleeing

Ephraimites to pronounce the password "shibboleth." If anyone pronounced the word incorrectly and said "sibboleth," he betrayed his Ephraimite origins and they were immediately killed (Judg 12:6). Every thought which cannot pronounce the name of Jesus or isn't harmonious with him, becomes like this, annihilated.

To stand watch on your heart in this way presumes a disposition of inner watchfulness. Those who live in a condition of spiritual sleepiness are in no condition to sift their thoughts. "You must be awake," writes Theofan, "and with sharp and implacable attention note all that takes place within you. As soon as an impulse crops up in your head, you should chase it away and battle it at close quarters in an active and spiritual way. At the same time, you shouldn't forget that in yourself you awaken and stimulate both the spirit of contrition and sorrow for your sins."[43] This need not be any sickly narcissism. This attention to "thoughts" is, rather, an expression of an inner and always wide-awake availability.

But just as much, thoughts are the feelings which attack us during prayer. For some the risk of being caught by them is even greater. The feelings can come. Psychology has taught us much about what damage can be caused by suppressed feelings. But we should not allow ourselves to be ensnared and trapped in them if we want to be open and receptive to God. He is so endlessly greater that what we can think or feel. An unselfish basic position is what frees us meeting him.

When we accept both thoughts and feelings in this freedom and with a firm resolve not to give way to anything in our innermost part than simple love, then the thoughts and the feelings can never hinder our nearness to God. The rule is meet and let go!

$\overline{7}$

Have Mercy on Me, a Sinner

In *A Book on Christian Deep Meditation*, I have emphasized that people ought to be more explicitly conscious about their Christian identity and constantly "remind themselves" that they share in divine nature. In the depths of our essence we are light.[44] Maybe one is surprised that the Jesus Prayer's tradition to such a high degree lays emphasis on man's sinfulness. Instead of "recognizing his worthiness,"[45] and rejoicing over it, he cries consciously about his sinfulness constantly to God's mercy. Is there a contradiction here?

That human beings are divine and at the same time sinners is one of the fundamental paradoxes of Christianity. But the true state of affairs is not that men are divine in one part of their essence and sinners in another part. Sin comes from having forgotten their true nature. The basic sin is actually this forgetting, this lack of consciousness and attention about the deepest truth about ourselves: that we are derived from God. The more conscious we are about our innermost essence, the more "destitute" the heart becomes (*cor contritium)* when we see what alienation we have lived in for so long and which we continue to live in.

Or in other words: The nearer we come to God, the more distinctly we see our weakness and sin in his light. Who has not experienced this? As soon as we begin to create order in our lives, we discover that the disorder is enormous and that we can never, by our own strength, fix it. Every attempt to create order causes new forms of disorder to arise, even more stubborn and difficult to master. Take, for example, love for one's neighbor. You begin by being loving toward everyone and not saying anything unfavorable about anyone. When you have once acquired this habit— who acquires it completely?—you do your best not even to think unfavorably about your neighbor. If you have come so far—who ever comes so far?—you try afterwards to no longer let yourself be led by emotional sympathy or antipathy and also to love your enemies, those whom you feel have wounded and irritated you. And while you make this fruitless attempt to attain this universal love, it becomes all the more apparent that what you thought was love was in reality selfishness. True love excludes no one, it loves each and every one of God's unique and absolutely irreplaceable creation.

Like the sun, it rises over both righteous and unrighteous (Mt 5:45). "For if you love those who love you, what reward do you have?" (Mt 5:46). In other words: What is such a love worth? It becomes more and more apparent that everything man has done has been infected with the virus of self-love. After you have for years climbed up the mountain of holiness, it ends with an unavoidable fall. And so it is that "the last state of that person is worse than the first" (Mt 12:45), so it appears.

In truth, a wonderful logic! Do everything you can so that at last you discover that you cannot do anything. But this kind of logic shows itself all the time on the spiritual paths. When Teresa of Ávila describes the prayer of rest, she challenges her Sisters to strive for this good: "You want immediately, my daughters, to reach as far as this prayer, and you are right in so doing. For, as I have said, the soul cannot completely understand what the Lord is doing for it and with what love he draws it nearer to himself. It is of course desirable to know how we can win this grace."[46]

Yes, how shall we actually win this grace? "Humility, humility," she writes. "In this way we let our Lord conquer, so that he hears our prayer. And the first sign that you have this humility is that you do not believe that you have earned the Lord's gifts of grace and delights or count on earning them as long as you live. You ask: how shall one in this way go forward to acquire them? To this I answer that there is no better way than the one I have told you, to not seek to acquire them."[47]

Those who have been brought up on Aristotle's logic feel a little uncomfortable in the face of this contradiction. And there are several of these in the works of Teresa. But the tension that they express is an important element in the Christian life.

Jesus' own life is a pertinent illustration of this. Jesus did all he could in order to announce God's kingdom for Israel, at the same time that he foresaw Israel not accepting his message. We see the same thing in the prophets. God commands them to preach a radical transformation, but at the same time he says that their work will be in vain. "Go," says the Lord to Isaiah, "and say to this people: 'Keep listening but do not comprehend, keep looking but do not understand.' Make the minds of this people dull and stop their ears, and shut their eyes, so that they may not look with their eyes, and listen with their ears, and comprehend with their minds, and turn and be healed" (Isa 6:9–10).

It seems to be a sign of God's pedagogy that he gives us a task which exceeds our powers. Through the hesitation which comes over us, when it becomes apparent that our strength isn't enough and complete failure is inevitable, something completely new can be born in us: a new insight about our destitution, a genuine humility, a limitless trust.

Martin Buber tells about a man who had sounded the depths of his weakness, and therefore only trusted in God. One day Rabbi Chaim stood and looked out through the window. He saw someone go by, and bade him come in. "Can you tell me," asked Rabbi Chaim, "what you would do if you found a purse filled with ducats? Would you give it back to its owner?" "Rabbi," the man replied, "If I knew the owner, I would immediately give him his money back." "You are a fool," said Rabbi Chaim. He returned to the window and called to another who went by and posed the same question to him. "I'm not so dumb," replied this one, "that I would give back a purse I had found." "You are a bandit, a proper scoundrel," said Rabbi Chaim, and called in a third person. This person replied: "Rabbi, how shall I be able to know what measure of justice will I have attained on this occasion? I cannot be certain that I will succeed in overcoming my desire for money. It is possible that the desire will overcome me and I will place the money in my own pocket. But maybe God—blessed be his Name—will come to extend grace and help me to give back the money I have found to its owner." "What a wonderful reply," cried Rabbi Chaim, "you have true wisdom."[48]

8

The Asceticism of Weakness

In this area, little Thérèse is the great teacher, and it is just this that has made her a Doctor of the Church—a title that confers the highest authority as a spiritual guide. The holiness of heroic greatness, which was the ideal in her time and place, she reshaped fearlessly into the holiness of destitution. Thérèse understood that true heroism consisted in that she completely accepted her poverty as a condition for complete trust. This insight was not the result of abstract reasoning. Thérèse sought a solution to a truly practical problem. She felt tormented by a limitless longing for holiness. Several weeks after her entry into a Carmelite cloister, she wrote to her father: "I will try to honor you by becoming a great saint."[49] In the face of this ideal, Thérèse felt her radical incapacity. But she discovered that love celebrates its greatest triumphs through grace, and it is weakness and misery which "unleash" God's grace. In order to move God's heart, she must have "empty hands." To the subprioress, Sister Fébronie, who was accustomed to dwell on God's righteousness, Sister Thérèse put it short and sweet: "Sister, you want God's righteousness, and you shall have it. The soul gets precisely what it expects of God."[50] For herself, Thérèse decisively chose grace.

Without knowing it, Thérèse connected herself to the great tradition of the Jesus Prayer. It cannot be in any other way, because the Gospels are the common source. "Those who are well have no need of a physician, but those who are sick; I have come to call not the righteous but sinners to repentance" (Lk 5:31–32). If you would draw the attention of the Lord to yourself, you must be small and weak. Those who think of themselves as splendid or strong have little to expect from Jesus.

Among all the forms of asceticism, the asceticism of weakness is the most important. The discovery of this is a decisive turning point in our lives. Everything that was an obstacle now becomes an aid, and all that formerly awakened dejection becomes a source of happiness and trust. In this way, we avoid the most dangerous of temptations: depression, melancholy. Someone who sought Rabbi Jakob Jizchak from Lublin complained that the evil thoughts which constantly beset him made him melancholic. Rabbi Jakob replied: "Be above all on guard against melancholy; it is worse and more pernicious than sin itself. When the evil spirit awakens bad thoughts, it is not its intention to lead men into sin but rather to get him, through sin, to lose courage."[51]

When you, in the deeper and deeper encounter with Jesus, with faith in his name, learn to confront your weakness in the right way, depression gives way to trust, tribulation becomes happiness. You know full well that God is happy when you give your sins to him. Your own and others. And that's fine. You don't need to buy God's love with good deeds. His love *is*, it is always there. If he loves you, it is not because you are good, but because he is good. It is not your deeds or successes which give you power over him, but your poverty.

Poverty makes you all-powerful, provided that you voluntarily show it to him. The strength for which you pray to God is not the kind of power that makes you strong. No. You pray to him rather for strength to be weak, not to flee from or conceal your fundamental weakness.

When Mother Agnes (Thérèse's own sister, who was also the prioress of her cloister) complained about her weaknesses to Thérèse, she received this reply: "Of course, I too am exposed to weakness, but this makes me happy—It is so nice to feel oneself weak and small!"[52] Earlier she had written: "O Jesus, how your little bird is happy to be small and weak; what would become of it if it were large?"[53]

Some years later, Consummata wrote: "I think that I am the more united with him the more wretched I feel. Instead of making me sorry, my wretchedness causes me to be filled with happiness, for the more unfulfilled I feel, the more his endless grace is opened for me. Just by seeing how far under all others I really stand, I understand how endlessly powerful his love for me is."[54]

This discovery is not made just once for everyone. On this road, we must constantly begin again. This is perhaps the deepest meaning in the repeating of the words "have mercy on me, a sinner" in the Jesus Prayer. One repeats constantly what one constantly forgets. To completely accept that one is and knows nothing is the most difficult thing there is. One must incessantly continue to impress this on oneself. But "miseria" (misery) and "misericordia" (mercy) are united in the Jesus Prayer into a happy couple. The tears which stream have shown this: it is the tears of repentance and at the same time the tears of thankful wonder.

Actually all prayer is a possibility to practice the ascetic of weakness. The prayer often gives us no satisfaction at all or no reason for pride. Those who "succeed" in the spiritual life, those who can glory in their will power and courage, should devote more time to prayer. There they would experience their weakness. Pope

John Paul II has spoken brilliantly about this: "Prayers are a strength for the weak and a weakness for the strong." We do not feel strong when, during prayer time, we are completely empty, without beautiful or deep thoughts, completely dry and cold. It is a matter of holding out, of not flying from this emptiness, not to want "to do" something. Instead of being disappointed we should be happy. In this poverty we are in the truth and thereby nearer God than if we had magnificent gifts to give him. God can only show his strength in and through our weakness.

The ascetic of weakness can be especially intense during a period of depression. But depression need never be fruitless. A friend wrote to me: "In depression I get a foretaste of the complete destitution of all that is mine, which I so inwardly long for that He can be *everything* in me. That pulls me out of the context where I am expected to function and places me in a position of total dependence. My strength to act is gone, my will enfeebled—and even my desire feels bound and stupefied. I am placed in a condition of practically pure vegetation. In this way I discover that only God still keeps me alive. Only He drives the blood through my arteries. Only He inspires my heart to beat—He teaches me to repose in my destitution and place all my hope in Him alone." The reasons for depression can be very different. Perhaps we have been really struck by a great sorrow. But it can also be physiological processes or the constitutional weakness of the psyche which bring about depression.

There is within us all a room which no depression— however it may come—can reach. We cannot simply by straining our will avoid the painful symptoms, in any event not completely. (We can of course do *something* to avoid giving nourishment to these symptoms.) But we can, by giving ourselves over to Jesus, be better able to discover this free room. There we meet him who has everything in his hand, also our depression and its causes. Prayer in fact makes life easier. Not by taking away all of the weaknesses, but by opening new spaces where everything becomes meaningful. Nothing needs to go lost in this life. In this way, a depression can provide a unique opportunity to exercise ourselves in weakness, and grow in reliance on God's mercy.

Our weaknesses can be a problem for those with whom we associate, and obviously we should try to avoid making life difficult for others. But the weakness which without self-pity is handed over pleases God as much as all the great works we can do. It is only before men that it looks so different.

Life is like a knitting, with knitting and purling stitches. We so often think that we must only have knitted stitches. But the result becomes monotonous. By also purling, the entirety can be more living. Thus, our life's purling stitches—mistakes and faults—amount to a part of our calling's special pattern.

In the Jesus Prayer one is far from the emphasis on strength of will which marked past generations. Perhaps this is one of the reasons why the Jesus Prayer is the "in thing" nowadays.

The persons of our time are psychically much weaker than their forebears. Many have deep wounds in their psychic structure as a result of lack of love during the time they grew up. Comfort contributes also to a growing weakness. We are less hardened and consequently also less resistant to life's physical and psychic stresses.

Because of this fragility, we are driven even more than our ancestors to an ascetic of weakness. The ascetic which emphasized will had as its goal to bend the will and make the strong weak. Contemporary man is already weak enough. The role which our ascetic should play is above all to teach us to accept our weakness and reshape it into a complete openness to God.

To accept and to affirm in no way excludes our own activity. It is obvious that work is necessary so that our whole being should be healthy and sound. And this on three planes: The physical, the psychic, and the spiritual. But while we are doing all that we can, we should accept that we cannot do everything and that we can never attain complete harmony.

It will always be that some flaws will remain. But they are flaws only in the cold eye of humankind; in the eye of Love, they belong to the special wholeness which makes up each and every one of us. Everything, absolutely everything, allows itself to be integrated, everything can play a positive role. The dissonances can contribute to harmony on a higher plane. A crease can make a dress ugly but it can also be an ornament. Thérèse of Lisieux writes about this with the words of Saint John of the Cross: "According to my experience, love is so powerful in deeds that it benefits from everything it finds in me, from the good as well as from the evil, and changes my soul into itself."[55]

All of our wounds, and those of the world can, like Jesus' wounds, be changed into glorified stigmata the nearer we are to him, bowing our knees at his name. Because he humbled himself and did not want to keep his greatness, taking the lowest of places from limitless love for each and all of us, just because of this, it is in his name that everything in heaven and on earth finds their true glory.

Notes

1. *The Philokalia* is an anthology of hesykastic prayers published in 1782 by Makarios of Corinth and Nicodemus Hagioriten.

2. These tales were published about 1870 in Kazan. In Swedish by Natur och Kultur, Stockholm, 1961. New edition, 1980.

3. Thérèse of the Infant Jesus. *Självbiografiska skrifter* (Autobiographical Writings), (Carmel series, nr 1, 1971) p. 177.

4. *Benediktijns Tijdschrift* (Benedictine Journal), Sint Adelbertabdij, Egmond-Binnen, 1979, I, p. 26.

5. Ibid, p. 24.

6. *Ökenfådernas tänkespråk* (Proverbs of the Desert Fathers), translated by Per Beskow, Artos 1982, p. 95.

7. PG, t. 88, kol 1112c.

8. *Les sentences des Pères du désert* (The Sayings of the Desert Fathers), I, Solesmes, 1966, p. 40.

9. Evagrios. *Antirhetikon*, philargyria 9. See also Anselm Grün, *Gebet und Selbsterkenntnis*, Vier-Turme-Verlag, Münsterschwarzach, 1979, pp. 43–44.

10. *Les sentences des Pères du désert* (The Sayings of the Desert Fathers), III, Solesmes, 1976, p. 141ff. See also A. Grün, aa, p. 46.

11. *Apophthegma* 298. See also A. Grün, aa, p. 46.

12. *Les sentences des Pères du désert* (The Sayings of the Desert Fathers), II, Solesmes, 1977, p. 64. See also A. Grün, aa, p. 46.

13. *Ökenfadernas tänkespråk* (Proverbs of the Desert Fathers), p. 93.

14. Ibid., p. 95.

15. *Ordstäv samlade av pater Eliseus av Martyrerna* (Sayings Collected by Father Eliseus of the Martyrs), 5, in *Levande Kärlekslöga och mindre skrifter* (Carmel Series, nr 15), 1984, pp. 227–228. See also P. M., *Mot det fulla livet i Karmel*, nr 1 (1971), årg 6, pp. 2–13.

16. Ibid.

17. Barsanuphe and Jean de Gaza, *Correspondance*, Solesmes, 1971, p. 227–228.

18. "Jesus is nothing if he is not Christ, and Christ is nothing when he is not Jesus," wrote Hans Urs von Balthasar on the cover of his translation of Henri de Lubac's book about Origen's interpretation of the Bible (*Geist aus der Geschichte*, Johannes Verlag, Einsiedeln, 1968).

19. Saint John of the Cross's poem *Jag vågade allt i en kärlekens flykt* ("I Dared All in a Flight of Love") in *Levande Kärlekslåga och mindre skrifter*, p. 183.

20. A Monk of the Eastern Church, *La prière de Jésus* (The Jesus Prayer), Chevetogne, 1963, p. 52.

21. Ibid.

22. Bokförkaget Catholica, 1996, nr 2563, p. 664.

23. See also Higoumène Chariton de Valamo, *L'art de la prière* (The Art of Prayer), Eastern Spirituality 18, Abbaye de Bellefontaine, Bégrolles en Mauges, 1976, p. 261.

24. *Sång av själen som fröhdar sug åt att känna Gud genom tron* (Song of the Soul That Rejoices in Knowing God

Through Faith), in *Levande Kärlekslåga och mindre skrifter*, p. 170.

25. *En rysk pilgrims berättelser*, (A Russian Pilgrim's Tale), p. 21.

26. Ibid.

27. Franz Jalics, *Kontemplative Exerzitien* (Contemplative Exercises), Echter Verlag, Würzburg, 1994.

28. *L'art de la prière* (The Art of Prayer), p. 129.

29. Ibid, pp. 140–141.

30. The title of number 14 in the series is "*Spiritualité orientale*," 1974.

31. *Andliga Skrifter* (Carmel series, nr 7), 1979, p. 87.

32. *En ryske pilgrim's berättele* (A Russian Pilgrim's Tale), p. 39.

33. Cited by Oliver Clément in *La Douloureuse joie* (The Painful Joy), p. 30.

34. Pp. 26–27.

35. Barsanuphe and Jean de Gaza, *Correspondance*, p. 59.

36. Thérèse of the Infant Jesus, *Självbuigrafiska skrifter* (Autobiographical Writings), p. 190.

37. Pp. 23–24.

38. In the first part of this book, p. 11.

39. *L'art de la prière* (The Art of Prayer), p. 64–65.

40. *Entretien avec Motovilov* (Interview With Motovilov), Spiritualité Orientale, II, p. 190.

41. *Bestigningen av Berget Karmel* (The Ascent of Mount Carmel), (Carmel series, nr 6) 1978, II, 12, 5, p. 113.

42. *Levande Kärlekslåga*, III, 38, p. 97.

43. *L'art de la prière* (The Art of Prayer), p. 336.

44. Libris, Örebro, new edition 1977, p. 32–41.

45. "Agnosce, o Christiane, dignitatem tuam," Leo the Great, *Sermo I* in *Nativitate Domini*, PL 54, col 193.

46. *Den inre borgen* (The Inner Fortress), (Carmel series, nr 3) 1974, IV, 2, 8, p. 62.

47. Ibid, pp. 62–63.

48. Martin Buber, *Die Erzählungen der Chassidim*, Manesse Verllag, Zürich, 1949, p. 697–698.

49. May–June (?) 1888. *Oeuvres Complètes*, Edition du Cerf, Paris, 1996, p. 346.

50. *Correspondance Générale*, Editions du Cerf, Paris, 1972, T II, p. 648.

51. *Die Erzählungen der Chassidim*, p. 476.

52. July 5. *Sista samtal* (Last Conversations), (Carmel series, nr 20) 1988, p 43.

53. *Självbiografiska skrifter* (Autobiographical Writings), p. 175.

54. *Lettres de "Consummata" à une carmélite*, Carmel d'Avignon, 1931, p. 135. Consummata, actually Marie Antoinette de Geuser (1889–1918), a French mystic who belonged to the Third Order Carmelites.

55. *Självbiografiska skrifter* (Autobiographical Writings), p. 56. See John of the Cross, *Glossa till det gudomliga* (A Gloss on the Divine).